To Ongalifu

I cannot t

for your support. Best wishes

to you.

[illegible] W. C[illegible]

2/18/97

WICKED WORDS

POISONED MINDS

RACISM IN THE DICTIONARY

FIRPO W. CARR, Ph.D.

Wicked Words: Poisoned Minds
Racism in the Dictionary

Edited by Erin Texiera
Cover designed by Lisa A. Doyle
Concept by Firpo W. Carr

ISBN Number 0-9631293-5-X

Scholar Technological Institute of Research, Inc. (S.T.I.R., Inc.)
Post Office Box 13752
Los Angeles, California 90013
(213) 857-8051

Printed by: Professional Press
Chapel Hill, NC 27515-4371

Picture Credits
Page 11, Jim Hubbard, 1991
Page 12, The Science Museum/Science & Society Picture Library
Page 33, *The World Book Encyclopedia*
Page 34, Harold Ritts
Page 55, Michael Newton
Page 56, *U.S. News & World Report*
Page 79, Harold Ritts
Page 80, *The World Book Encyclopedia*
Page 97, Unknown
Page 98, AP/Wide World Photo
Page 115, Unknown
Page 116, Unknown
Photo of author on inside right flap, Camille Denise

Manufactured in the United States of America
00 99 98 97 96 10 9 8 7 6 5 4 3 2 1

"There is one whose rash words

are like sword thrusts."

—Proverbs 12:18, *Revised Standard Version*

ACKNOWLEDGMENTS

I offer many heartfelt thanks to my family, intimate circle of friends, and students who supported me throughout the entire, agonizing ordeal of building, writing, crafting, and fashioning this book. After being turned down by agent after agent and publisher after publisher, I decided the only way to get this book into the hands of the public was to publish it myself.

Amateur proofreaders and editors donated precious time because they believed in the cause behind the writing of such a book. I owe them all a debt of gratitude. Finally, I thank Jehovah God for the gift of life itself, and the confidence of knowing that some day soon he will erase the very specter of racism from our persona.

Preface

In September 1994, with unsuspecting thoughts, I embarked upon a casual reading of the dictionary—*Webster's Ninth New Collegiate Dictionary* (1991) to be exact. What started as a casual read turned into an intense research effort that produced the present work. What I discovered was stunning. The dictionary carefully conceals many racist words.

One way employed by racists to keep blacks and whites in the dark, is to lock them in what amounts to be a cold, deep, dungeon of ignorance. In actuality, it's worse than that.

Through the dictionary, flagrantly biased editors replace ignorance with bad, faulty, inaccurate knowledge. They do it with a smooth, silky subtlety. They pull us out of the dark only to have us bask in, what is in reality, deadly artificial sunlight.

Even when they aren't massaging and manipulating definitions in the dictionary to support their ideas, they are carefully omitting pertinent information that might be considered damaging to their cause.

A word of caution, however, is called for. All the editors aren't guilty. Some have done an exceptional job. Regrettably, others have created an us-versus-them category that leads to divisions and racism.

Ironically, they have spoon-fed us the very thing they designed the dictionary to combat—ignorance. The dictionary, that bastion of language, the ultimate word authority, instead, helps us to remain a divided and racist society. This is a shameful commentary on the bedrock of our literary world.

I don't feel qualified to offer an alternate definition for the offending words. I am not an editor, although in a few instances I offer a suggestion or two. I suppose I could recommend "marriage" over the racially divisive expression "mixed marriage"; "nursemaid" instead of the offensive word for a black woman "mammy"; or "dancer" in favor of "jig," the insulting term for a black dancer.

Nevertheless, that's not my job. My purpose in writing this book is to expose the shocking, dehumanizing racism that permeates the dictionary.

Obviously, I'm not the only one who feels this way. The dictionary's racism has shocked others. *The San Diego Union-Tribune* of Saturday, May 20, 1995 carried an article entitled, "In a word, this gadget is offensive."

The article stated that Walt Roston "purchased an English-Spanish translator late last month at the Radio Shack store in the College Grove shopping center.

"While learning to use the palm-sized device at his home, the African-American social worker discovered that one of its English translations for the Spanish word *negro*—meaning 'black'—is the racial slur 'nigger.'

"'I was disgusted. I couldn't believe it,' said Roston, who bought the $30 machine to help him communicate with Hispanic people in his work as an eligibility officer at the county's welfare facility."

When Roston complained to the store management, they added fuel to the fire. "They told me," he said, "it was a common word found in the dictionary." This is precisely why I am writing this book. Dictionary editors have been extremely irresponsible and insensitive.

Is what happened to Mr. Roston an isolated case? Absolutely not. The *Los Angeles Times* of Saturday, July 6, 1996 printed this startling news:

"Microsoft Apologizes for Offensive Synonyms: The Redmond, Wash.-based software company issued a public apology for the Spanish-language version of a Word 6.0 thesaurus that offered 'savage' and 'man-eater' as synonyms for the name 'Indian.' Reports of the offensive synonyms surfaced in Spain and Mexico, where they caused a media uproar."

Countless other incidents happen in print on a daily basis. Ultimately, the guilty ones who use offensive words embrace the dictionary as their scapegoat. True, such racist reasoning stems from the root, the infrastructure of our language—the dictionary itself. But, I have news for you: The root is rotten to the core.

If I sound angry, it's not meant to be intimidating. The dictionary disturbed me when I noticed what it said about blacks. Actually, the dictionary itself accurately describe my feelings. Surprisingly, there's an entry for "angry young man" in *Webster's Ninth New Collegiate Dictionary*. He's defined as "an outspoken critic of or protester against an economic condition or social injustice."

While I wouldn't dare claim to be "an outspoken critic" for the entire black race, I am "against . . . social injustice." I suspect that societal inequities unsettle most people.

Webster's Ninth New Collegiate Dictionary isn't the only offending dictionary. In varying degrees, wicked words and thoughts are found in *Merriam Webster's Collegiate Dictionary—Tenth Edition (1993-1994), The Merriam Webster Dictionary* (1994), the comprehensive 20-volume set of *The Oxford English Dictionary (1994),* and the *American Heritage Dictionary of the English Language, Third Edition (1992).*

All of the offending words, phrases, or expressions have been first categorized and then alphabetized. I examined Encyclopedias, medical books, and other reference works. For the most part, I have consulted books from the 1990s only. Surprisingly, these works either expose biases in the dictionaries mentioned above, or are biased themselves.

Am I expecting perfection in speech from imperfect people? Certainly not. That wouldn't be reasonable. "No one can [completely] tame the human tongue," writes a Christian Jew from 20 centuries ago. "It is an evil always liable to break out and the poison it spreads is deadly." (James 3:8, *The New Testament in Modern English,* by J.B. Phillips) Yes, the "human tongue" will occasionally spew wicked words and "the poison it spreads is deadly." But this is NO REASON to endorse, document, memorialize, or institutionalize racism in the pages of the dictionary!

In conclusion, since the Constitution of the United States of America is based on the Judeo-Christian ethic, a scripture discussing "words" will grace the beginning of each chapter. As you read this book, I'm sure you'll decide for yourself whether wicked words from the dictionary have poisoned our minds.

TABLE OF CONENTS

I. Racism and Black Essence

"Does not the ear test words
and the mouth taste its food?"
—Job 12:11, *The New King James Version*

●

Just as we taste food before we consume it, our ears should "test" words before we swallow the definition. Some definitions are rotten to the core and will make you sick! Scientific experiments tell us that our minds take longer to process offensive words. These words actually stun the mind! James Moffatt's translation asks: "Does not a man's mind test what he is told?" See if your mind tests out these words:

Aryan: *a member of the Indo-European-speaking people early occupying the Iranian plateau or entering India and conquering and amalgamating with the earlier non-Indo-European inhabitants.—Webster's Ninth New Collegiate Dictionary.*

An Aryan is a racist white person who hates blacks, Jews, immigrants, and others. White Aryan Resistance (WAR) is the name of a white supremacist organization that regularly commits hate crimes. *Webster's Ninth New Collegiate Dictionary* doesn't tell us any of this.

The *Oxford English Dictionary* says regarding "Aryanism": "Under the Nazi regime (1933-45) [it] applied to the inhabitants of Germany of non-Jewish extraction."

The *American Heritage Dictionary* candidly states that an Aryan is "in Nazism, a Caucasian Gentile, especially of Nordic type." The German Nazis considered themselves Aryans or the master race.

Literature in Germany in the 1930s and 1940s used the word regularly. Statements like "The Founder of the Christian faith...was of 'Aryan' not Jewish descent" (1940), and, "The town...was cleared of its 'Aryan' population and made a centre, or rather a concentration camp, for all Jews" (1943), are just a couple of examples.

Despite the fact that the historical Aryans invaded India from the north and disrupted her culture, and despite the fact that atrocities were committed against the Jews, and others, in the name of Aryanism, the Sanskrit word for "Aryan" means "noble, of good family." It's stunning to know that *Webster's Ninth New Collegiate Dictionary* completely eliminates the racist nature of "Aryan" in its definition.

The definition in *Webster's Ninth New Collegiate Dictionary* empowers white supremacists to get away with openly calling themselves the Aryan Brotherhood or some other such name that could intimidate blacks that may be working on the job with them. It's a demoralizing reminder to any black person that the entire "system," even the very dictionary itself, is against them.

(NOTE: What *Webster's Tenth* Says: It finally adds the words "used in Nazism to designate a supposed master race of non-Jewish Caucasians having esp[ecially] Nordic features." Why didn't they say this in the first place?)

black-a-moor: *a dark-skinned person; esp[ecially]: NEGRO.—Webster's Ninth New Collegiate Dictionary.*

This term was invented because the Moors, who were black, conquered Spain—a *white* European country. To this day Spain doesn't have much use for black people.

"Black-a-moor" is a nonsensical expression. According to the *Oxford English Dictionary* "no satisfactory explanation has been offered" regarding its etymological significance.

At the root of the term "black-a-moor" is the word "Moor." The *Oxford English Dictionary* gives an interesting history of the word "Moor" in its first definition:

"In Ancient History, a native of Mauritania, a region of Northern Africa corresponding to parts of Morocco and Algeria. In later times, one belonging to the people of mixed Berber and Arab race, Muslim in religion, who constitute the bulk of the population of North-western Africa, and who in the 8th c[entury] conquered Spain.

"In the Middle Ages, and as late as the 17th c[entury], the Moors were commonly supposed to be mostly black or very swarthy (though the existence of 'white Moors' was recognized), and hence the word was often used for 'Negro'...blackamoor."

Again, historians tell us that the Moors were black. Shakespeare illustrated this fact in his play The Tragedy of Othello, The Moor of Venice. Othello was clearly a black man. These same black Moors conquered white Spain. White racist history cannot stand this fact. So, they changed it by creating "white Moors."

To prove this, notice that the *Oxford English Dictionary* says that the "Moors" were "*supposed* to be mostly black." Did you also notice that the editors made it a point to mention that there were "white Moors" also? The implication is that these fictional "white Moors" were the ones that conquered white Spain.

According to the *Oxford English Dictionary* a "black-a-moor" is "a black-skinned African, an Ethiopian, a Negro" or "any very dark-skinned person."

In actuality, "black-a-moor" is an offensive, racist term. The second definition in the *Oxford English Dictionary* says that a "black-a-moor" is "a devil."

In listing the expression "black-a-moor," dictionaries rob blacks of what shreds of pride or self-worth they desperately try to cling onto. These racist-based dictionaries are telling black people: "You have contributed nothing to history. And don't believe for a moment that you could had ever conquered *any* white race!"

Cajun (or Cajan): *...a Louisianian descended from French-speaking immigrants from Acadia; one of the people of mixed white, Indian, and Negro ancestry in southwest Alabama and southeast Mississippi.—Webster's Ninth New Collegiate Dictionary.*

The racist nature of this word is particularly subtle. Whenever a dictionary entry includes "Negro ancestry" in its definition, but also applies exclusively to whites, that word or expression is sanitized.

In other words, normally, any word that suggests "Negro ancestry" contains offensive elements in its definition. But if that same word describes *whites only* somewhere in the definition, all bad elements are taken out. It's no longer an offensive word. This is the case with "Cajun."

As the above definition states, Cajuns came from Acadia. The region of Acadia was located in eastern Canada and was the first European colony in North America. Acadians were white, so, although this word applies to a mixed-race person who also has black blood in him, the definition is cleaned up. (See also "Creole" below.)

Given the "one drop" rule, the meaning of "Cajun" is confusing. The "one drop" rule, which originated in the South, states that anyone with at least "one drop" of "Negro" blood in his veins is "Negro"; it doesn't matter how white he looks.

Elizabeth Atkins Bowman of *The Detroit News* says that "[t]he *one drop* rule originated as a way for slave owners to enforce strict boundaries of class and race between whites and blacks and it persists in law. As recently as 1986, Louisiana upheld a law that classifies anyone with 1/36 black blood as black." (Compare "miscegenation" in Chapter III.)

This is the first word listed in the dictionary that "fractionalizes" (breaks down into fractions) black people. No other race is ever divided up into measured blood components.

So, if you're under the white part of "Cajun," you have nothing to fear. But if you're black, forget it—you're a "Caged One."

(NOTE: What *Webster's Tenth* Says: It excludes the words "one of the people of mixed white, Indian, and Negro ancestry in southwest Alabama and southeast Mississippi.")

Caucasian: *of or relating to the white race as classified through physical features; of or relating to the white race as defined by law specif[ically] as composed of persons of European, No[rth] African, or southwest Asian ancestry.—Webster's Ninth New Collegiate Dictionary.*

Though we are lead to believe that this word refers to white people, white racism dictates that it be used to describe blacks when blacks perform in a way that defies the derogatory way in which whites normally portray them.

In other words, when a few blacks perform in a superior fashion, they are termed "Caucasian." In this way, the rest of the black race will always be viewed as subhuman.

Did you know that certain Northern Africans are considered "Caucasian"? As you'll see later, it gets even more convoluted than this. But first, let's consider the North Africans.

White Europe and America have determined that peoples from the African countries of Ethiopia and Egypt (both North of the equator) are Caucasian. There are two reasons for this: (1) The ancient Egyptians built the pyramids (which defy modern technology); (2) Ethiopia soundly defeated a European country, Italy, in 1895.

First, according to white racist thinking, black Africans of Egypt weren't smart enough to have built the pyramids, so, with the stroke of a pen, they're "white." The same is true with the Ethiopians. There's no way that Black Africans can defeat a European power. So, Ethiopia, you're now "white." A brief historical review will explain what happened.

Toward the end of the 19th century, Italy proudly declared itself the protector of Ethiopia as if it owned the beautiful African country. When this peaceful nation refused to go along with this unilateral arrangement, Italy sent troops to force its will on the Ethiopians. The Italian forces were thoroughly routed, thereby forcing them to recognize Ethiopia as its own independent nation.

But, according to "the powers that be," only white people can defeat white people, so, again, with the stroke of the pen, this Black African nation was turned white, or, described as "Caucasian." (On certain job applications in the U.S. that have race classifications, there are separate designations for "Negro" and "Ethiopian." Unfortunately, some Ethiopians don't consider themselves "Negroid.")

But, amidst the recategorization of Ethiopians, there's a secret disdain of these Africans on the part of those who christened them with Caucasianhood. You see, they were never quite forgiven for mangling the Italians who attacked them. (See "Ethiopian" in Chapter III.)

Even in Russia, there's a strange sort of irony associated with the word "Caucasian." To demonstrate how confusing the word "Caucasian" can be in today's rapidly changing global climate, consider the following:

The *Los Angeles Times* (April 8, 1995) carried a front-page article entitled "In Russia, Fertile Soil for Racism," which started by saying:

"Shock troops stormed into a Moscow marketplace last month, rounded up all the dark-skinned males and herded them onto a bus, using rubber truncheons to silence anyone who complained."

Can you believe that these "dark-skinned" people were called, of all things, "Caucasians"?

The *Times* reports that not many people are alarmed by "the stereotyping, scapegoating and harassment of a 'dark' people, the Caucasians." You see, they're from the southern section of Caucasia, a region of the former Soviet Union.

Is it really fair to say that the black Caucasians are treated like African-American descendants of slaves? One dark-skinned Caucasian woman complained: "We're just like 'blacks' to [white Russians]. We speak their [Russian] language and read their [Russian] literature, and they still regard us as savages from the south."

The article further stated that prior to the fall of communism, "racism was viewed as a capitalist evil." For the black man, racism is a capitalistic evil; a socialistic evil; a universal evil.

Creole: *a person of European descent born esp[ecially] in the West Indies or Spanish America...a white person descended from early French or Spanish settlers of the U.S. Gulf states and preserving their speech and culture...a person of mixed French or Spanish and Negro descent speaking a dialect of French or Spanish...the French dialect spoken by many Negroes in southern Louisiana; haitian.—Webster's Ninth New Collegiate Dictionary.*

As is the case with the word "Cajun," the racist nature of this word is particularly deceptive. Since one of the definitions of the word "Creole" applies exclusively to whites, there's no derogatory connotation—even though "Negro descent" is part of the definition.

It's simply the second word in the dictionary that fractionalizes the black man. (See "Cajun" above for more details.)

mulatto: *the first-generation offspring of a Negro and a white; a person of mixed Caucasian and Negro ancestry.—Webster's Ninth New Collegiate Dictionary.*

Unlike the words "Cajun" and "Creole" (a person who has a little "Negro" blood in him), a "mulatto" has too much (50%) "Negro" blood in him! Because of this, a negative, racist connotation is given to "mulatto." It's derived from the Spanish word that means "mule" and is the third word considered in the present work that fractionalizes the black man.

Historically, as mentioned earlier, Spain, like other European countries, hasn't been kind to black people. Former Spanish colonies, employing the language of Spain, have followed suit. *Newsweek* magazine (February 13, 1995) provides background as to the basis for this allegation:

"An array of Latin American terms have arisen to describe various racial combinations, with the most pejorative ones reserved for people of dark hue and pelo malo—or bad (meaning kinky) hair. Status in some Latin societies is so linked to color that mejorando la raza (bettering the race) is taken to mean marrying someone lighter in order to have whiter children. Uruguayan writer Eduardo Galeano observes: 'In the Dominican Republic there are a lot of black people, but you never see *black* listed as skin color on their identity card....It would damage the possibilities for work, for a social life.'"

Other dictionaries list the words "hybrid," "cross-breed," "mongrel," and "half-breed" as synonyms for "mulatto." You'll notice that all these terms apply to animals. When you have too much "Negro" blood in you, you become like him—an animal.

Do you think that the offspring of a "mixed [black and white] couple" should be compared to an animal?

Furthermore, two mules cannot breed and bring forth offspring. The very term is a contradiction in that two so-called "mulattos" can indeed produce yet another beautiful, healthy human being.

No doubt such a definition was designed to discourage marriage *and* pregnancy between blacks and whites. In the twisted reality of the white racist, if the mixed coupled were to have a baby, it would be considered black. Even our children's minds have even been poisoned with this nonsense.

In one study, groups of adults and children were shown four photographs of couples holding a baby whose face wasn't showing. There was a white couple, a black couple, a black man with a white woman, and a white man with a black woman.

"When asked what race the babies would be," states Elizabeth Atkins Bowman of *The Detroit News,* "second- and fifth-graders had varying answers, but 12-year-olds and adults believed overwhelmingly that the baby would be black."

Another expression directly related to "mulatto" is "high yaller." *Webster's Ninth New Collegiate Dictionary* candidly describes this term as "a mulatto or Negro of light-brown color—called also high yellow; often taken to be offensive."

So, although "mulatto" and "high yaller" are synonymous, "high yaller" is listed as offensive while "mulatto" is totally acceptable.

Finally, black people are made to feel that their blood actually contaminates, like some incurable virus, the blood of whites. White racists tell everyone who'll listen that even one drop of black blood is potent enough to change your race to black.

Sadly, the resulting impact on the unsuspecting black mind is one of self hatred. And if the person is a cursed "mulatto," he or she may be rejected by both blacks and whites.

(NOTE: What *Webster's Tenth* Says: In an effort to correct this glaring inconsistency, *Webster's Tenth*, under the new entry "high yellow" says: "a black person of light complexion—called also high yaller ... often taken to be offensive." You'll notice the comparison to "mulatto" was taken out.)

Negro (Negroes): *a member of the black race of mankind distinguished from members of other races usu[ually] by inherited physical and physiological characteristics without regard to language or culture; esp[ecially] a member of a people belonging to the African branch of the black race; a person of Negro descent.—Webster's Ninth New Collegiate Dictionary.*

A "Negro" is specifically a black person of African descent—for the moment. Why "for the moment"? Because white racist opinion shapers define and redefine the word as they see fit.

How do they determine if you're a "Negro"? It all hinges on how much "Negro" or Black African blood your bone marrow produces. In other words, they try to determine how much "black" blood your heart pumps through your body. And keep in mind, this is "without regard to language or culture," according to the above definition.

"We are the only race that's fractionalized in this manner, for purposes other than noble ones" complained one black educator. "What if a white person received several pints of blood in a blood transfusion from a black person? Is that white person now black?"

As we ponder this question, notice how a recent *Newsweek* magazine article (February 13, 1995) tackled the issue: "In

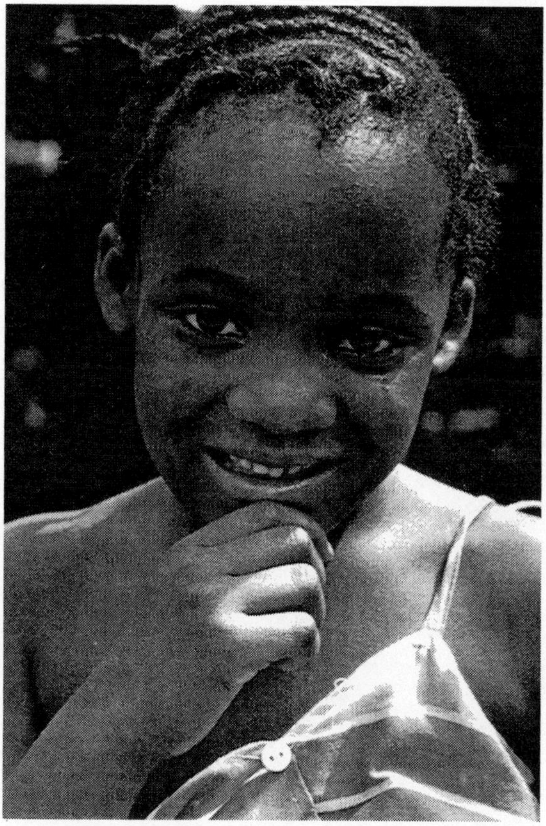

A **pickaninny** is a black child or "the offspring of an animal" according to the dictionary. Black infants are more than twice as likely to die than white ones. (See page 43 under "pickaninny.")

Hitler's **Aryans** think of themselves as a master race of whites who are superior to every other race. Though they hate Blacks, Jews, and others, the dictionary neglects to mention this. (See "Aryan" on page 1.)

America—still—one drop of 'black blood' is enough to change one's complexion....As F. James Davis, a sociologist and author of *Who Is Black?* observed, 'other racial minorities...can be absorbed if they become one-fourth or less of that ancestry.'

"But because people are so accustomed to classifying anyone with any African heritage as black, he says, most Americans 'don't even think' to view blacks the same way as other immigrant groups....In Virginia during the 1800s, someone with less than one-fourth 'Negro blood' could be white.

"In 1910, the state codified what had already become custom: white was defined as having less than one-sixteenth 'Negro ancestry.' By 1924, urged on by white supremacists, legislators prohibited whites from marrying anyone with 'a single drop of Negro blood.' Other states, in the North as well as in the South, adopted a similarly restrictive view."

This same revealing article went on to say that "[t]hough many of the racial-classification statues no longer exist, the tradition continues. As recently as 1986, the U.S. Supreme Court let stand a lower-court ruling forcing a Louisiana woman with negligible African heritage to be legally defined as black."

So, this whimsical definition of "Negro" (a serious attempt to define the very essence of a man) is left to an arbitrary white American system that really, from a historical standpoint, has no use for the black man.

And if the black man refuses to surrender his very nature, his soul, to people who view him as a subhuman enemy, he is branded a "militant," or "black nationalist." And if he dares to think he should be treated humanely, as a white person for instance, he is called a "New Negro."

The *Oxford English Dictionary* defines "New Negro" as "a Negro claiming equal status with a white American." Imagine that.

Of course this implies that the "Old Negro" was one who knew his subservient place in white American society.

But, just how is a "Negro" really defined? What are his physical characteristics? The *Oxford English Dictionary* really breaks it down for us:

"An individual (esp. a male) belonging to the African race of mankind, which is distinguished by a black skin, black tightly curled hair, and a nose flatter and lips thicker and more protruding then is common among white Europeans. [Why the comparison with white Europeans? Why are they the implied standard for normalcy?]

"In the nineteenth and twentieth centuries [it] also applied (now somewhat less frequently because of the increasing use of the word Black) to individuals of African ancestry born in or resident in the United States or in other English-speaking countries. (Now customarily written with a capital initial.)...[Compare] New Negro [and] nigger."

Well, there you have it, in living color (or, is it black and white?) Remeber, ultimately, a white person is "white," "as defined by law," according to the definition for "Caucasian" discussed earlier. How will "Negro" be defined in the future? It all depends on how certain whites feel. And, if anyone asks you are you a "Negro," simply respond: "It all depends."

(NOTE: What *Webster's Tenth* Says: It adds the words, "sometimes taken to be offensive." We're moving in the right direction now. Interesting note, the words "of mankind" are taken out of the above definition.)

non-white: *(1927) a person whose features and esp[ecially] whose skin color are distinctively different from those of Caucasians of northwestern Europe; esp[ecially] one who has African ancestors of the black race.—Webster's Ninth New Collegiate Dictionary.*

Did you notice that the term "non-white" means "especially one who has African ancestors of the black race"? That's exactly what "non-white" really means: black people. They, in particular, are singled out.

The *Oxford English Dictionary* defines the above term as "not having white skin; or pertaining to people who are not white." The wording is very general here. The clauses "not having white skin" and "pertaining to people who are not white" are vague at best. They can include any number of "non-white" peoples. In fact, these terms are nothing more than smoke screens. By "non-white" they really mean black people.

This becomes strikingly apparent when we consider the expression "white man's burden." (See Chapter II.) According to *Webster's Ninth New Collegiate Dictionary*, it's "the alleged duty of the white peoples to manage the affairs of the less developed nonwhite peoples." What they're really saying is "the less developed nonwhite peoples" are African nations, though other non-African nations may be included.

So, does this mean that black people should come up with the expression "black man's burden" meaning "the inescapable burden of being black in the white man's world?" Should "non-black" also be an expression?

Nubian: *a native or inhabitant of Nubia; a member of one of the group of Negroid tribes that formed a powerful empire between Egypt and Ethiopia from the 6th to the 14th centuries.—Webster's Ninth New Collegiate Dictionary.*

Neither the word "Negroid" nor the word "tribes" is politically correct these days. (As discussed later under "tribe" in Chapter II, it suggests that which is primitive, backward, archaic.) To its credit, *Webster's Ninth New Collegiate Dictionary* doesn't define the "Nubian" through the eyes of the ancient Greeks as it did the word "Ethiopian" discussed in Chapter III.

Despite how powerful an empire the Nubians had, the *Oxford English Dictionary* makes it a point to describe a Nubian as "a native of Nubia; a Nubian slave." Were the Nubians really black? Absolutely. The *British Cyclopedia* (1836) said "the Nubians..have the thick lips..[and are] of the Negro race."

It may come as a no surprise to some who believe that since the Nubians were a highly civilized, organized and powerful group of Black Africans, their entry in a dictionary (Webster's 1994 pocket size edition) that boasts of being, in their own words, "America's #1 Paperback Dictionary," would somehow be omitted.

(NOTE: What *Webster's Tenth* Says: It removes the words "Negroid tribes" from the above definition and substitutes the term "dark-skinned peoples." The editors leave us guessing as to why they've taken this action. It's a good move nonetheless.)

octoroon: *a person of one-eighth Negro ancestry. —Webster's Ninth New Collegiate Dictionary.*

They forgot something. An "octoroon" is "a [*white*] person of one-eight Negro ancestry." The *Oxford English Dictionary* bears this out when it describes an "octoroon" as "a person having one-eighth negro blood; the offspring of a quadroon [one-fourth black] and a white." This is the fourth word that fractionalizes the black man.

The *Oxford English Dictionary* goes on to quote one source back in 1862 that says "the mulattoes [half-black, half-white], quadroons [three-quarters white, one-quarter black], and octoroons [seven-eighths white, one-eighth black]...now form so large a portion of the enslaved population of the South." In other words, at that time, there were very few full-blooded Black Africans. They now had various fractional "niggers."

These words were born out of the slavery period—more precisely, during the Civil War. They are all very offensive. And of particular interest is the fact that there are no well-known words (if any at all) for fractional blood mixtures between whites and peoples of other races.

quadroon: *a person of one-quarter Negro ancestry. —Webster's Ninth New Collegiate Dictionary.*

Something's missing. The definition should really read: "a [*white*] person of one-quarter Negro ancestry." Who's responsible for this term? We can thank the Europeans, the Spanish specifically, for introducing us to our fifth word that fractionalizes the black man.

According to the *American Heritage Dictionary* a "quadroon" is "a person having one-quarter Black ancestry."

The *Oxford English Dictionary* says that a "quadroon" is "one who is the offspring of a white person and a mulatto; one who has a quarter of Negro blood....One who is forth in descent from a Negro, one of the parents in each generation being white."

The word "quadroon" itself (just like "mulatto," "octoroon," and others) is revolting. The definition clearly implies the following: "You're one quarter nigger! That makes you all nigger!" Notice, please, that a "quadroon" isn't called "three-quarters white," or some other non-black race.

No, the emphasis is on a supposed disqualifier: one quarter black. Are there words for "one-quarter white" and "one-eighth white" where the remaining portion of blood is black? Not in a million years. The fact that there isn't drains the self-esteem from the souls of black folks.

Rhodesian man: *an extinct African man (Homo rhodesiensis or Africanthropus rhodesiensis) having long bones of modern type, a skull with prominent brow ridges and large face but human palate* *and dentition, and a simple but relatively large brain.—Webster's Ninth New Collegiate Dictionary.*

Yes, "Rhodesian man" is "an extinct African man." Some might say even the original man. But, just to keep black people in line, *Webster's Ninth New Collegiate Dictionary* unnecessarily adds the words: "a simple but relatively large brain." None of the other major dictionaries adds these words.

The fact of the matter is, the African skull mentioned in the above definition is older and larger than another one found in Europe. Simply put, racist white people don't like this fact. So, what do they do? They say: "Yes, it's larger, but, it's simple." "Ours," they gleefully continue, "has a complex skull which indicates that it has a more complex brain."

Of course, this is the pitiful, shallow fantasy of the desperate racist mind. The implications are serious. Of all the fleshy creatures on earth who have brains, man has the largest.

If there's a correlation to brain size and intelligence (which there isn't; a male's brain is generally larger than the female's brain but he certainly isn't more intelligent), that would make "Homo Africanthropus" (mentioned in the definition) more intelligent. The white racist certainly can't stand for that.

A recent scientific discovery contributes further to the anxious quandary, the dreadful dilemma of racists: DNA testing suggests that man originated in Africa.

The *Los Angeles Times* (May 26, 1995) states: "Emory University geneticist Douglas Wallace recently calculated that modern humans left Africa about 130,000 [years] ago, settled Asia about 75,000 years ago, reaching East Asia about 94,000 years ago and Europe about 79,000 years ago." The international scientific community agrees.

"[T]he Genetics Institute of Japan," continues the article, "suggested that modern humans left Africa about 143,000 years ago, reaching East Asia about 94,000 years ago and Europe about 79,000 years ago."

Continuing further, "a Stanford Medical School expert on human genetics and evolution...suggests that modern humanity left its African homeland a mere 112,000 years ago....

"Scientists say it is only a matter of time, and additional genetic archeology, until they can prove not only that modern males evolved from a common ancestor, but also that he was African in origin."

This information is surely distressing to anyone with thoughts of white racial superiority.

And for those who believe that the races evolved separately (called the "multiregional hypothesis"), the consensus of the scientific community says "our numbers come out very much against that."

In fact, they say, as the Bible has stated for millennia, that all races of man have a common ancestor. But, let's get back to a noteworthy irony regarding "Rhodesian man."

"Rhodesian man" was named after a British financier and imperialist named Cicel John Rhodes. The *Oxford English Dictionary* defines "Rhodesian man" as "a fossil hominid usually considered to be an early type of Homo sapiens, known from remains found in Broken Hill, Northern Rhodesia, in 1921."

The *American Heritage Dictionary* describes "Rhodesian man" similar to *Webster's Ninth New Collegiate Dictionary*, but without the racist, degrading words, "and a simple but relatively large brain."

It defines him as "[a] fossil human...found in south-central Africa, having a large low skull with massive brow ridges and skeletal bones like those of modern human beings."

Actually, in paleontology, "Rhodesia man" was discovered in Africa, consistent with what's stated above, and shouldn't be named after a European white man. This suggests the stain of European ownership.

The Europeans already have an early fossil (younger than "Rhodesian man") named after them; it's called the European Neanderthal Man. Rhodesian Man's real name should probably be "Homo Africanthropus."

By the time you read this, it's likely that some "reclassification" of things may have occurred, or, some "new" discoveries that will no doubt continue to perpetrate the racist agenda.

Blacks have seen their motherland raped by Europeans. And, now, they've dug up African ancestral bones and defiled black heritage by stripping them of their identity.

(NOTE: What *Webster's Tenth* Says: It changes "African man" to "African hominid." This effectively confuses most readers and blurs the image of the black man. It also removes the term "Africanthropus rhodensiensis" which detracts from any scientific endorsement of the African origin of "Rhodesian man.")

Semitic: *of, relating to, or constituting a subfamily of the Afro-Asiatic language family that includes Hebrew, Aramaic, Arabic, and Ethiopic.—Webster's Ninth New Collegiate Dictionary.*

This term has become almost exclusively Jewish. It shouldn't be. Being "Semitic" doesn't mean just being Jewish. It also means being Arabic, and Ethiopian. Obviously, Ethiopians are black Africans, so, according to the above definition, a black African, if he's Ethiopian, is Semitic.

The *Oxford English Dictionary* says that "in the linguistic sense" it's "the distinctive epithet [or, racist word] of that family of languages of which Hebrew, Aramaen, Arabic, Ethiopic, and ancient Assyrian, are the principal members." So, again, it's not just a Jewish epithet ("a disparaging or abusive word or phrase").

For those who believe otherwise, we ask this thought-provoking question: When an Ethiopian immigrant, a black African, was killed by skinheads in Washington state, was that, more specifically, an anti-Semitic act aside from being a hate crime? Yes, it was "anti-Semitic," if we are to believe the above definition.

The *American Heritage Dictionary* says that it's "[o]f, relating to, or constituting a subgroup of the Afro-Asiatic language group that includes Arabic, Hebrew, Amharic, and Aramaic." Notice that both Webster's and the *American Heritage Dictionary* link the word "Semitic" with "Afro-Asiatic."

(NOTE: What *Webster's Tenth* Says: It replaces the word "Ethiopic" with "Amharic." This move evokes mixed emotions. The bad news first. "Ethiopian," from which we derive "Ethiopic," was meant to be an insulting term. It basically means "burnt" (not "dark") faces. (See "Ethiopian" in Chapter III.) Also, substituting "Amharic" for "Ethiopic" confuses the reader since most people don't associate the Amharic language with Africa. Now for the good news. "Ethiopic," also known as Classical Ethiopic (or Ge'ez), is an ancient language of the Coptic church that is no longer spoken by the masses in Ethiopia. As mentioned, they speak Amharic, a Semitic language. This makes for an accurate update.)

II. Every Day Racist Slurs

"How long will you exhaust me
and pulverize me with words?"
—Job 19:2, *The New English Bible*

♠

Racist words crush the soul. Don't believe the old adage: Sticks and stones may break my bones but words will never hurt me. Words can leave bruises and the deepest of emotional scars. The saying should be: Sticks and stones may break my bones and words will *ever* hurt me. Notice these words:

anti-black: *(1952) opposed or hostile to people belonging to the Negro race <his anti-black attitude>.—Webster's Ninth New Collegiate Dictionary.*

So all black people are "Negroes"? It appears that this definition is especially designed to single out the North American "Negro."

All "black" people, as the definition implies, aren't "Negroes." In India, as well as other places in the world, there are people with very dark skin who obviously don't belong to members of what has been socially or traditionally described as the "negroid" race.

Additionally, one not familiar with American history could easily get the impression that anti-black sentiments didn't occur until 1952, the year the term first appeared in print. On the other hand, one could be left with the thought that "anti-white" (as seen below) feelings occurred as far back as 1906, hinting, of course, that these feelings were harbored at that time by descendants of slaves in the United States.

Finally, the *American Heritage Dictionary* puts it the way it should be: "Hostile or opposed to Black people." The example it uses? "Many...are...trying to mitigate their...anti-black attitudes...by forming a renewed identification with 'blackness' and the ghetto" (Alvin F. Poussaint). This conciliatory example is much more refreshing than the one found in *Webster's Ninth New Collegiate Dictionary*.

Please refuse the urge to believe that "anti-black" is the same as anti-Negro, although *Webster's Ninth New Collegiate Dictionary* hints at this conclusion. "Anti-black" means being against anyone who is black or dark-skinned. It doesn't mean everyone who is just a "Negro."

So, in conclusion, if you're a white person who can't resist being "anti-black," please hate all black or dark-skinned people, not just "Negroes." Of course, you'll have a lot of people to hate since the dark-skinned or non-white peoples of the world far outnumber the white people of the world.

(NOTE: What *Webster's Tenth* Says: It defines "anti-black" simply as being "opposed or hostile to black people." Okay. That's better.)

anti-Semitism: *(1881) hostility toward or discrimination against Jews as a religious or racial group.—Webster's Ninth New Collegiate Dictionary.*

"Why is it that this term is restricted to the Jews when there are other Semitic races?" pondered one scholar. One might guess that the unspeakable horrors perpetrated against Jews in the Holocaust have something to do with it.

"But, the term was used decades before the Holocaust," this same scholar retorts. "Is a subtle form of racial superiority inherent in this expression?"

There are numerous Semitic languages and peoples. (See "Semitic" in Chapter I.) For reasons that are unknown to the author, "Semite" came to be synonymous with "Jew." How it came about that the Jews claimed exclusive use of the word "Semitic" remains a mystery and will perhaps remain entangled in debate.

If someone is a hater of Jews or Jewish people, the appropriate term should be "anti-Jew" or "anti-Jewish," not the all-encompassing term "anti-Semitic."

That this point is salient can be demonstrated by a religious irony involving the Ethiopians. The Jews themselves, in the light of recent events, can be called "anti-Semitic." (Remember, the term "Semitic" includes an "Ethiopic" "subfamily" according to Webster's.)

After claiming to be the "lost tribe" of Israel and subsequently being rejected by the Ethiopian government, the Israeli government airlifted black-skinned "Ethiopian Jews" to Israel.

After caring for their needs initially, rampant racism reared its ugly head. The Ethiopians found that orthodox Judaism summarily rejected their form of Judaism.

The *Los Angeles Times* (January 30, 1996) says that Ethiopic Judaism "was not accepted by the rabbinate in Israel. [Ethiopian religious] leaders, called *kessim,* were not recognized, and Ethiopian men, in particular, were made to go through ritual conversions that they found insulting because they felt they had kept the faith for millennia without anyone's seal of approval."

This rejection even affected the Ethiopian's right to an honorable marriage. The same article continues by saying that "[b]ecause [the Ethiopians] were not considered 'real Jews,' they found it difficult to marry in Israel, where there is no civil marriage."

The *Los Angeles Times* (January 29, 1996) quotes Mazel Zana, an 18-year-old Ethiopian female who lives in the Israeli town of Beersheba, as saying: "All the white people in Israel are racist. In Ethiopia, we had to fight because [of] and for our Judaism."

So, we ask: Are these Jews being anti-Semitic? By definition, Yes, if what Mazel Zana says is true. (See "Ethiopian" in Chapter III.)

In any event, *Webster's Ninth New Collegiate Dictionary* is very kind to Jews everywhere insofar as definitions are concerned. In fact, it's flagrantly biased toward Jews. This is born out under the definition of "Tay Sachs disease," as discussed in Chapter IV. Surprisingly, there isn't a term called "pro-Semitism" or "pro-Jewish" in *Webster's Ninth New Collegiate Dictionary*.

anti-white: *(1906) opposed or hostile to people belonging to a light-skinned race.—Webster's Ninth New Collegiate Dictionary.*

Two things become immediately apparent: (1) instead of just being of "the white race," any person of "a light-skinned race" is included under the category of "white"; (2) the term "anti-white" isn't used in a negative example as the term "anti-black" is (i.e., most good blacks are really anti-white).

The definition in *Webster's Ninth New Collegiate Dictionary* sends this message out: Not just white people, but all "light-skinned" people should beware of black people who are "anti-white."

Fortunately, again, the *American Heritage Dictionary* comes to the rescue. It gives a straightforward, unbiased definition with a positive example. It defines "anti-white" as follows: "Hostile or opposed to white people." The example? "To talk about black doesn't mean we are anti-white" (Ron Clark).

We are given a mitigating example that easily allays fears and hopefully encourages dialogue between blacks and whites.

So, light-skinned "Negroes" (and others), please don't fear that when someone is "anti-white," they are including you in their generalized hatemongering. Be relieved to know that they probably just hate white people.

bete noire: *(1844) a person or thing strongly detested or avoided: bugbear.—Webster's Ninth New Collegiate Dictionary.*

The black African was a beast in the minds of European whites. Without a doubt, this term is a veiled reference to the black man, even though a black person isn't mentioned anywhere in the definition. It's a French expression that literally means "black beast."

In fact, in 1902 a book was published bearing the title *The Negro A Beast*. Not everyone agreed with this characterization. In that very same year, Charles Taze Russell, a well-known white minister, countered with an article entitled "The Negro Not a Beast," which appeared in the July 15, 1902 issue of *Zion's Watch Tower*.

European whites weren't the only ones calling Africans "black beasts." Their white American brothers joined them in taunting the black man. The American press even went so far as to publicize horrible news of the terrifying murder of "black beasts" for other than noble purposes.

Notice this *Oxford English Dictionary* reference from 1922 England: "*Black Beast Burned in Omaha, Ga.* A lot of Deadwood Dicks in slouch hats [fired] at a sambo [a derogatory term for a black man; see "sambo" below] strung up on a tree with his tongue out and a bonfire under him."

In plain English, this refers to white racists shooting at the dead body of a black man hanging from a tree with a fire lit under him. The dead man was referred to as a "Black Beast"—French, "bete noire."

Additionally, you'll notice the word "bugbear" in looking at the above definition. The *Oxford English Dictionary* describes "bugbear" as "a sort of hobgoblin (presumably in the shape of a bear) supposed to devour naughty children; hence, generally, any imaginary being invoked by nurses to frighten children."

Guess who was depicted as the "bugbear" in the children's story? The black man. But, he wasn't imaginary. He was very real. So, little innocent white children went to bed having nightmares of black men, and subsequently grew up being terrified of them—especially big ones.

The term "bugaboo" refers to a black man also. This is an offensive word. The *Oxford English Dictionary* describes it as "a fancied object of terror; a bogy [which means "the evil one, the devil"], a bugbear."

The *Oxford English Dictionary* introduces yet another racist word related to "bugaboo." Under "jigaboo," it reads: "Related to jig...after bugaboo. A Black person, a Negro."

"Bete noire," "bugbear," "bugaboo," "jig," and "jigaboo," are all damning references to the black man, who, according to the above definition of "bete noire," is seen to be "a person or thing strongly detested or avoided."

So, when you see Magic Johnson trick opposing players with his moves on the basketball court, or Michael Jordan defy gravity as he soars effortlessly through the stratosphere for a slam dunk, or Shaquielle O'Neal rip down rims and shatter backboards with his thunderous, monster-like dunks, keep in mind that they are nothing more than "black beasts," according to a veiled reference in *Webster's Ninth New Collegiate Dictionary*.

black: *...having dark skin, hair, and eyes ... of or relating to a group or race characterized by dark pigmentation; esp : of or relating to the Negro race ... or relating to the Afro=American people or culture ... DIRTY, SOILED ... characterized by absence of light ... thoroughly sinister or evil : wicked ... indicative of condemnation or discredit ... connected with or invoking the supernatural and esp. the devil ... very sad, gloomy, or calamitous ... marked by the occurrence of disaster ... characterized by hostility or angry discontent : SULLEN.—Webster's Ninth New Collegiate Dictionary.*

In Spike Lee's 1992 movie depicting the life of Malcolm X, Malcolm, as played by actor Denzel Washington, read the entire dictionary while in prison. One scene showed Malcolm comparing the definition of the word "black" with all its associated negativism, with the word "white" with its mostly positive connotations.

When Malcolm entered the Norfolk, Massachusetts, Prison Colony in 1948, he read the above definition. Sad to say, not much has changed.

One has only to look closely at how "black" people are dismally defined and compared to a "dark," incarnate "evil"—"the devil" himself. Being "black" means to be "dirty, soiled." It means to be "thoroughly sinister [which means "left-handed"] or evil; wicked."

Finally, according to *Webster's Ninth New Collegiate Dictionary,* to be "black" means to be "characterized by hostility or angry discontent." The definition, in its totality, speaks for itself. (Please compare to the definition for "white.")

black English: *a nonstandard dialect of English held to be spoken by American blacks.—Webster's Ninth New Collegiate Dictionary.*

First of all, all American blacks don't speak this "black" or "nonstandard" English. This is a regrettable generalization. Anyway, why single out this type of English? Is "Spenglish," English spoken with a strong Mexican-Spanish accent, listed in *Webster's Ninth New Collegiate Dictionary*?

What about other forms of "nonstandard" English spoken by Chinese-Americans ("Chinenglish"), Korean-Americans ("Korenglish"), Japanese-Americans ("Japenglish"), Italian-Americans ("Itenglish"), etc.? Are there dictionary terms for these? No way.

Oh, sure, these "types" or "forms" of English are spoken by people whose first language is one other than English. That was also true of African slaves, but with a difference: They involuntarily learned the language of their slave masters.

To add insult to injury, "White English" is defined in the *Oxford English Dictionary* as "the English of white speakers." There's no mention of it being "substandard" or "nonstandard," even though many uneducated whites (like "hillbillies") speak a dialect of English that is certainly substandard. But, again, there's no word in any major dictionary for substandard "White English."

Actually, many believe that "nonstandard" Black English is a form of revolt against racist white people and their English language. It's the black man's way of saying: "I'm going to slaughter your language since you abuse me with it."

All the other ethnic groups desired to learn English, and that under pleasant conditions, as opposed to the inhumane, unimaginable conditions surrounding slavery.

No, "Black English" certainly isn't the King's English. Yes, "Black English" is nonstandard. But, so were the conditions under which Black English was born. Slavery, too, was "nonstandard."

(NOTE: What *Webster's Tenth* Says: It redefines "black English" as follows: "a nonstandard variety of English spoken by some American blacks." Notice the addition of the word "some.")

coon: *(1742) raccoon; negro—usu[ally] taken to be offensive.—Webster's Ninth New Collegiate Dictionary.*

Make no mistake about it. This is an offensive term for any black person, and especially a black man. And please don't allow *Webster's Ninth New Collegiate Dictionary* to delude you into thinking that this term "usu[ally]" offends black people. It doubtless offends most blacks most of the time.

Interestingly, the grammar-checking personal computer program called Grammatik, when used to check this book, stopped on the word "coon" and displayed the following: "Offensive: Avoid this offensive term. Consider revising."

The *American Heritage Dictionary* pointedly states that this is an "offensive slang [that is] used as a disparaging term for a Black person." You'll notice the word "usually" isn't used here.

Given what we now know about Webster's dictionaries, it shouldn't be surprising to know that *The Merriam Webster Dictionary* (1994) defines "coon" as simply "raccoon." This mistakenly suggests it's no longer offensive to call a "Negro" a "coon."

The *Oxford English Dictionary* candidly admits that the word "coon" is a disparaging slang for "a Negro." It gives the example of an article in the *Chicago Defender* (October 23, 1948) where a black man complained: "A lot of us are referred to as 'nigger,' 'coon,' 'darky,' etc., right to our faces."

Beautiful black songs, as well as handsome and beautiful black singers, were called "coon songs" and "coon-shouters" respectively. The *Oxford English Dictionary* says these terms fell into disuse "because of their offensiveness." One wonders why the same thing didn't happen to the word "coon."

ghetto: *(1611) a quarter of a city in which Jews were formerly required to live; a quarter of a city in which members of a minority group live esp[ecially] because of social, legal, or economic pressure.—Webster's Ninth New Collegiate Dictionary.*

In the minds of many people the words "ghetto" and "black" go together like milk and cookies. Some may be surprised to know that "ghetto" first originated with the Jews in 1611. (See also "Warsaw Ghetto" in your encyclopedia.)

Today, the word is synonymous with economically depressed black neighborhoods with high crime rates. It's misleading to think that this word, in its modern-day context, is associated with any other minority group.

For example, in the large North American cities of New York, Los Angeles, and San Francisco, numeric minorities like the Chinese, Koreans, or Jews have Chinatown, Koreatown, or the Jewish "section" (or "neighborhood") respectively. None of these, including the Jewish section, is called a "ghetto." (Spanish speaking neighborhoods in the Southwest US are called "barrios.")

Writers have long associated the "ghetto" with Black America. Consider the following by author Maya Angelou: "The needs of a society determine its ethics, and in the Black American ghettos the hero is that man who is offered only the crumbs from his country's table but by ingenuity and courage is able to take for himself a Lucullan feast."

Late author James Baldwin (1924-1987) wrote the following referring to children from the "ghetto": "All over Harlem, Negro boys and girls are growing into stunted maturity, trying desperately to find a place to stand; and the wonder is not that so many are ruined but that so many survive."

Additionally, Douglas S. Massey and Nancy A. Denton, in their book *American Apartheid* (1993), say that about 33% of all blacks live in racially segregated "ghettos."

So, although it happened mysteriously, the word was lifted off the backs of Jews and thrown on the backs of blacks, as if the latter didn't have enough to carry already. No one should have to carry that load.

This leads us to a paradox: Should we ask lexicographers to put the black man somewhere in the definition of "ghetto," or should we ask politicians to take him out of the ghetto? Whether these are the right questions, or whatever the answers are, the painful truth (at this point!) of the matter is this:

To leave any reference to "African American" or "black people" (or, God forbid, "Negro") out of the definition for "ghetto" is irresponsible, inconsistent, and a glaring omission. This criticism, to be sure, is stated reluctantly.

The veracity of this argument, nonetheless, is unquestionable. This is born out by the following definition of "ghetto blaster."

ghetto blaster: *a large portable radio or tape player that is often played loudly in public places.—Webster's Ninth New Collegiate Dictionary.*

A ghetto blaster is something that came out of the black neighborhood—the black "ghetto." The above definition suggests that a black person with a "ghetto blaster" is guilty of disturbing the peace, being a public nuisance, and perhaps loitering. The very definition indicts him.

Blacks should not be incriminated for loving music. And the term "ghetto blaster" should not automatically be associated with them. But, unfortunately, some blacks have bought into the stigmatism of being associated with the "ghetto blaster." *The New*

This is a gorilla, "an ... ape ... of western ... Africa." But, according to this same dictionary (please turn page)

...this beautiful black African woman, and any African-American woman, is also a "gorilla." (See "gorilla" on page 69.)

York Times, in its May 30, 1982 issue, tells us of a black rhythm and blues group called the "Ghetto Blasters." People got a clue that they were black just from the name.

The *Oxford English Dictionary* says that the term is an American slang for "a large portable stereo radio (and cassette player)... on which (Black) popular music is played loudly."

Whether it's something to brag about or be ashamed of, the "ghetto blaster" finds its origin in the black neighborhood, better known these days as "the 'hood.'"

(NOTE: What *Webster's Tenth* Says: It refers the reader to the "boom box" entry. There it defines "boom box" as "a large portable radio and often tape player with two attached speakers." Because it became popular with white youths, *Webster's Tenth* removes the words "often played in public places" from the previous definition of "ghetto blaster" in *Webster's Ninth*.)

golliwog: *a grotesque black doll; a person resembling a golliwog.—Webster's Ninth New Collegiate Dictionary.*

"A person resembling a [grotesque black doll]" is a black man. *Webster's Ninth New Collegiate Dictionary*, with the greatest of subtlety, skillfully validates this word by making no reference to "a Black male" in its definition. It's "officially," no longer a bad word.

The *American Heritage Dictionary* and the *Oxford English Dictionary*, respectively, put in what *Webster's Ninth New Collegiate Dictionary* leaves out. They say it's "[a] doll fashioned in grotesque caricature of a Black male. A name invented for a black-faced grotesquely dressed (male) doll with a shock of fuzzy hair." You can't put it any plainer than that.

As recently as 1969, during the Vietnam War, one writer from the British publication *British G.I. in Vietnam* described a black man as follows: "A short, slightly built negro whose appearance reminded me of one of those golliwogs that decorated the labels of Robertson's marmalade jars."

This flagrant attack on the appearance of the black man is not only unjustified, its dehumanizing. "Even when he goes and fights the white man's war he's treated like a dog," complained one black Vietnam veteran. "And people wonder why we're always demanding self respect."

jig or jigg: *any of several lively springy dances in triple rhythm; music to which a jig may be danced.—Webster's Ninth New Collegiate Dictionary*.

Although it doesn't appear to be at first glance, this is a very racist, offensive word for a black man. *Webster's Ninth New Collegiate Dictionary* just carefully omitted the offensive part so that the word could still be acceptably used in the U.S.

Thankfully, the *Oxford English Dictionary* forthrightly says exactly how the term, which originated in the U.S., is understood. It says it's an American slang for "[a] Black person, a Negro...a term that gives offence."

The word also carries stereotypic overtones. Consider this printed text, from 1932 England, regarding a type of job perceived by the public to be specifically for black men: "Janitor jobs were for jiggs." That is, for black men.

What about the cultured segment of English society? What would be their view of, say, Shakespeare's play The Tragedy of Othello, The Moor of Venice? "This jig we call Othello falls in love with this girl." This is how an Englishman described Othello in 1935.

Finally, someone might say, in accord with the definition given in *Webster's Ninth New Collegiate Dictionary*, that "jig means music and dancing, and, for some reason, black folks are known for their music and dancing." This statement, heard over and over again, isn't only a generalization, but another dig at the "jig."

Although Michael Jackson can sing and dance outstandingly well, the white racist will tell you that he is just one of the multitalented Jackson "jigs."

(NOTE: What *Webster's Tenth* Says: It adds a third definition to "jig" and defines it as follows: "jig [short for jigaboo black person] (1927); black—usu[ally] taken to be offensive.")

jigaboo: *a Black person, a Negro ... a term that gives offence.—Oxford English Dictionary.*

Webster's Ninth New Collegiate Dictionary doesn't list this word at all. Why not?

It could be that the editors realized that this word is just too offensive and, thus, totally unacceptable. This would be giving *Webster's Ninth New Collegiate Dictionary* the benefit of the doubt, but, unfortunately, there isn't much basis for that.

More than likely, the editors of *Webster's Ninth New Collegiate Dictionary* thought that entering "jigaboo" in their dictionary would be too flagrant and opprobrious. They listed "nigger" and probably felt that listing "jigaboo" would just be too much. They still got a punch in by listing the offensive term "bete noire" (discussed earlier) which is connected with "jigaboo." (Also see "jig" above.)

Kaffir or Kafir: *(1552): archaic: a member of a group of southern African Bantu-speaking peoples...often not cap[italized], chiefly So Afr[ican]: an African Negro—usu[ally] used disparagingly.—Webster's Ninth New Collegiate Dictionary.*

Simply put, this is the South African word for "nigger." And it's not usually "used disparagingly" as *Webster's Ninth New Collegiate Dictionary* puts it. It's *always* "used disparagingly."

The *American Heritage Dictionary* states: "Offensive. Used especially in southern Africa as a disparaging term for a Black person ... Islam...An infidel."

According to the *Oxford English Dictionary*, the word "Kaffir" not only applied to all Black Africans, but also to a white man who showed kindness toward them.

It states that it was "[u]sed disparagingly, with reference to any Black African; transf[ormed], as a term of [contempt], a white man who associates with or is thought to favour Black Africans."

It's the equivalent to the term "nigger lover" which is applied to white people who sympathize with or assist black people in their struggles. It's often used in the U.S., but especially in the Southern states where slavery existed. (See "white Negro" below.)

mammy: *a black woman serving as a nurse to white children esp[ecially] formerly in the southern U.S.—Webster's Ninth New Collegiate Dictionary.*

Even though *Webster's Ninth New Collegiate Dictionary* doesn't say it, this word is offensive. The *Oxford English Dictionary* basically says the same thing: "In the southern United States, esp[ecially] before the abolition of slavery: A coloured woman having the care of white children."

The *American Heritage Dictionary* is more honest. It says that "mammy [is] [o]ffensive. A Black nursemaid, especially one formerly in the southern United States."

Mohock: *(1711) one of a gang of aristocratic ruffians who assaulted and otherwise maltreated people in London streets in the early 18th century.—Webster's Ninth New Collegiate Dictionary.*

A rich gang of white males! This gang existed long before the Crips, Bloods, Black Stone Rangers, and other predominantly black gangs in the U.S. Credit *Webster's Ninth New Collegiate Dictionary* for listing this word.

The "Mohocks" even existed before the gangs headed by Al Capone and Dutch Schultz of the Roaring Twenties; the real originators of "drive-by shootings."

The *Oxford English Dictionary* says that these Mohocks "infested the streets of London at night in the early years of the 18th century." They gave true meaning to the term "gang-infested neighborhood."

To give us an idea of just how notorious these Mohocks were, one British writer from London, in 1711, asked her readers: "Did I tell you of a race of [degraded persons], called the Mohocks, that play the devil about this town every night, slit peoples noses, and beat them, etc.[?]"

So, when someone complains to you about gang warfare in black neighborhoods, know that "ganstas from the original 'hood,'" the "Mohocks," did it before them and that such behavior isn't confined to one race. (Compare "tong" in Chapter V.)

nigger: *(1700) NEGRO—usu[ally] taken to be offensive; a member of any dark-skinned race.—Webster's Ninth New Collegiate Dictionary.*

This word isn't "usu[ually] taken to be offensive." It's *always* "taken to be offensive"!

The *Oxford English Dictionary* simply says that a "nigger" is "a Negro," as if these terms were synonymous, hence, acceptable.

Portugal spearheaded the African slave trade. We shouldn't be surprised that the word "nigger" is of Portuguese origin. Incidentally, Brazil, a former Portuguese colony, was the last country in the Western Hemisphere to abolish slavery in 1888.

The *American Heritage Dictionary* says frankly that the word "nigger" is an "offensive slang" that's "used as a disparaging term for a Black person."

It carries such a negative connotation that its use has expanded beyond black people. The *American Heritage Dictionary* further states: "Used as a disparaging term for a member of any socially, economically, or politically deprived group of people." "Gun owners," for example, "are the new niggers . . . of society" according to writer John Aquilino.

Mr. Aquilino may identify gun owners as the "new niggers ... of society," but, let's not forget that the old "niggers" are still "niggers"—at least to many whites.

Regarding this conclusion, James Baldwin offered these encouraging words to the black man: "You can only be destroyed by believing that you really are what the white world calls a nigger."

(NOTE: What *Webster's Tenth* Says: It adds an entire section under "usage" which states: "Nigger ... can be found in the works of such writers of the past as Joseph Conrad, Mark Twain, and Charles Dickens, but it now ranks as perhaps the most offensive and inflammatory racial slur in English. Its use among blacks is not always intended or taken as offensive, but, ... it is otherwise a word expressive of racial hatred and bigotry." Hallelujah! Why didn't they say that in the first place?)

nig-nog: *A foolish person, hence, a raw and unskilled recruit; [shortened form of Nigger] ... A coarsely abusive term for a Negro.—Oxford English Dictionary.*

This term isn't found in *Webster's Ninth New Collegiate Dictionary*. America's motherland, Great Britain, has its own version of the extremely derogatory word "nigger." It's "nig-nog." It's, as the definition states, a "shortened form of nigger."

The late English comedian Benny Hill reportedly used the term "nig-nog" a number of times on one of the shows aired in both the United Kingdom and the United States. Though black people were being depicted, most African Americans had no idea that they were being offended.

ofay: *a white person—usu[ally] used disparagingly.—Webster's Ninth New Collegiate Dictionary.*

Although they've used it in the past, blacks didn't come up with this racist word for whites. This should be clearly stated in the definition, even though many blacks and whites aren't even aware of the word.

An expression similar to "ofay" is found in one of the chief white European languages. Some believe it's "ofay's" root. The *Oxford English Dictionary* gives us more details.

It says in 1936 "[t]he word ofay, which may have come from the French *au fait* (signifying mystery), is in general use in the Negro press of the United States to designate a white person."

But, the *Oxford English Dictionary* also says that "American Blacks" (journalists to be exact) used 'ofay' and that it was "an offensive term for 'a white person.'" Granted. "American Blacks" used it in the past, but not necessarily with a negative connotation.

If you look carefully, you'll notice that the *Oxford English Dictionary* doesn't say it was used *disparagingly* by "the Negro press of the United States."

Some linguists believe "ofay" is of African origin. They say it could be Pig Latin for "foe-is," or the Ibibio word "afia" which means "white or light-colored." Yoruba-speaking people of Africa would say "ofe" to protect themselves from danger.

After considering these possibilities, the *American Heritage Dictionary* says the Yoruba word "ofe" "was then transferred to white people, regarded as a danger to Black people throughout the wretched days of slavery and beyond"!

In examining the complete definition of "ofay" in the *American Heritage Dictionary*, you'll notice that it uses qualifying phrases like "possibly of West African origin" or "some scholars think [it was] borrowed from an African source." And finally, after admitting that the "source has not been pinned down," the expression "suggested possibilities" is used. These qualifiers could be seen as an attempt to place the blame on blacks for "ofay's" origin.

The *Oxford English Dictionary* reluctantly admits that the speculative reasoning identifying the source of "ofay" as being African "seems no more than an implausible guess." It appears to be the implausible guess of whites with racist tendencies.

So, blaming the black man for coming up with the supposedly offensive word "ofay" for the white man is a sham, a farce, a lie. And who's perpetrating this farce? Dare we say, racist "ofays"?

peckerwood: *a rural white southerner—often used disparagingly.—Webster's Ninth New Collegiate Dictionary.*

Historically, rural white southerners were (some still are) the most obvious of white racist bigots. Some of them belonged to the Ku Klux Klan and were/are responsible for terrorizing and killing a number of blacks. Right or wrong, these whites were differentiated by the term "peckerwood."

A close look at history also reveals that blacks have had no equivalent for white supremacist groups like the Ku Klux Klan who systematically harass, intimidate, and murder. Invariably, these white supremacists back up their name-calling with action. Note the following incident of a hate crime as reported in the April 29, 1995 issue of the *Los Angeles Times*:

"Peckerwoods...[a notorious gang of white males] takes its name from an old epithet some blacks use to refer to whites." Again, contrary to what the article implies, there's little or nothing to suggest that the term originated with blacks. The article goes on to say that three members of this gang did a "drive-by" on three young black men and the one-year-old daughter of one of them in Antelope Valley, California.

It seems that white supremacists wish to keep the word alive. The meaning, though, has expanded to include white bigots who aren't rural white southerners.

pickaninny: *a Negro child—often taken to be offensive. —Webster's Ninth New Collegiate Dictionary.*

Is there an offensive term for a white child? What about a Hispanic child? a Japanese child? Happily, there are none that the author is aware of. There is one, however, for the black child: pickaninny.

Interestingly, the grammar-checking personal computer program called Grammatik, when used to check this book, stopped on the word "pickaninny" (just as it did for the word "coon" discussed earlier) and displayed the following: "Offensive: Avoid this offensive term. Consider revising."

Black babies are the only babies (as far as the author knows) who have their own special derogatory term! As we'll see, racist language and attitudes easily translate into death for the beautiful African American child—this "pickaninny" as racists call him.

The expression comes from the Spanish word *pequeño* ("small") and is related to the Portuguese word *pequeno* ("little"). As far as the word "pickaninny" is concerned, they're talking about a "small" or "little" "Negro" person—an innocent black child in this case, as opposed to a black midget, dwarf, or lilliputian.

The *American Heritage Dictionary* says "pickaninny" is an offensive word "[u]sed as a disparaging term for a young Black child." Though it comes from the Spanish and Portuguese languages, it isn't confined to them. The European nations in general use this term.

The *Oxford English Dictionary* says it's "[a] little one, a child term (which now often gives offence when used by people of European extraction) [that] refers in the West Indies and America to children of Black African ethnic origin; in South and Central Africa and in Australia to those of the aboriginal peoples; in the latter cases introduced by Europeans."

A surprisingly frank confession. But it doesn't stop here. The *Oxford English Dictionary* also tells us that the word means "in Australia, and South and Central Africa...the offspring of an animal."

Once again, black babies are compared to "the offspring of an animal." Yet another word that endeavors to tie black people, young and old, to animals.

The situation is more serious than the targeting of helpless black babies by white racists. The attitude behind the racial slur has lead to shocking black infanticide.

Consider this fact: According to an article entitled "Infant Mortality as a Social Mirror" which appeared in the *New England Journal of Medicine,* June 4, 1992, black babies were more than twice as likely to die as white babies.

Basing her comments on a similar article, Farai Chideya, in *Don't Believe The Hype,* says "[a]ccording to the National Center for Health Statistics, in 1987 a stunning 11,461 of the 38,408 babies who died before their first birthday were black. Poverty isn't the only cause for the high black death rate.

"Even black middle-class families suffer higher mortality rates, according to a study of black and white families where both parents had attended college. Suspected causes behind the mortality gap include a lifetime of shoddy medical care, lack of prenatal care and—most telling—the chronic stress of being black in America."

Finally, it's demoralizing to know that, even if the black child lives, he has a bevy of belittling names awaiting him, as he grows up in a white world that hates him, and is determined to keep him on the "endangered species" list.

pimpmobile: *an ostentatious customized luxury car characteristic of a kind used by a pimp.—Webster's Ninth New Collegiate Dictionary.*

Who thought of this word? What possible point could there be to having this in the dictionary? While there are a few white pimps, when most people surveyed heard the word "pimp" they thought of black men, there "stables" (whores), and the ghetto.

Proportionately speaking, there are far more black men in jail for "pimping" (and crimes associated with it) than white men. It's almost an exclusively "black" crime. Historically, the "pimpmobile" was almost always a luxury car of some sort, although it could be any car nowadays.

Is there a term for cars that white criminals use that imply race, class and criminal status in one fell swoop? For example, are there "klanmobiles"?

The *American Heritage Dictionary* defines "pimp" as "one who finds customers for a prostitute" and "pimpmobile" as "a flashy, oversize automobile used by or deemed suitable for use by a pimp." But, remember, pimps are usually black. This is how many law enforcement officers see it.

Illustrating this, the August 23, 1995 issue of *The New York Times* states that former Los Angeles Police Department Detective Mark Fuhrman not only used the word nigger(s) "nearly 60" times in a taped interview, he associated nigger with "[his] favorite targets: Gang members, dope dealers, [and] pimps."

(NOTE: What *Webster's Tenth* Says: It rewords the definition saying that a "pimpmobile" is "an ostentatious luxury car of a kind characteristically used by a pimp.")

pommy or pommie: *Austral (1915) briton; esp: an English immigrant, often used disparagingly.—Webster's Ninth New Collegiate Dictionary.*

Due to nationalistic pride, there's even white-on-white name calling. This word, as well as others in the dictionary, demonstrates the veracity of the old saying, "man has the mastery over another to harm him."*—The Modern Language Bible: The New Berkeley Version in Modern English.*

The *American Heritage Dictionary* says that the word "pommy" in Australia and New Zealand is "used as a disparaging term for a British person, especially a recent immigrant." It also gives a brief history of the word by saying that it's "short for pomegranate, alteration of Pummy Grant, probably alteration of immigrant."

The *Oxford English Dictionary* states that it's "a derogatory term for an immigrant from the United Kingdom; an Englishman or Englishwoman, a Briton...(often a term of affectionate abuse) in Pommy bastard."

(NOTE: What *Webster's Tenth* Says: It capitalizes the word(s) and removes "often" from the definition. This hasn't happened with offensive words for black people. The bias continues.)

poor white: *a member of an inferior or underprivileged white social group—often taken to be offensive.—Webster's Ninth New Collegiate Dictionary.*

Where's "trash"?! The popular expression is "poor white *trash.*" The editors apparently couldn't bring themselves to call any white person "trash," so, they simply said "poor white."

The *American Heritage Dictionary* says that the term "poor white" is an offensive one and is "used as a disparaging term for a member of a class of low-income white farmers and laborers, especially in the southern United States." To be sure, America's poor white farmers have suffered trials and tribulations.

But, before you run off to join a white supremacist group like the Ku Klux Klan, or sympathize with their "white power" rhetoric, realize that these members "of an inferior or underprivileged white social group" were always considered to be better than, well, "Negroes."

In other words, no matter how "poor" or 'trashy' they were, they were still "white." That was all that mattered. How can we be so confident? Easy. Just consider the term "grandfather clause," considered in detail in Chapter V.

It's defined as "a provision in several southern state constitutions designed to enfranchise poor whites and disfranchise Negroes." That says it all. Poor southern whites were empowered by law to be better off politically and economically than black people.

Now, this isn't to say that individuals who fall under the classification of "poor white" as defined by the dictionary harbor racists beliefs. Some do. Some don't. This isn't an indictment of innocent, good-natured persons belonging to that group.

We are, however, pointing the finger at those whites who are responsible for documenting in law and literature the idea of white superiority including the insidious, sneaky, sly, slick and wicked definition above.

How does the British *Oxford English Dictionary* handle the expression "poor white"? It doesn't. It isn't listed at all. Apparently, the English editors would have none of that. While they "responsibly" carry words that are demeaning to Africans and their ancestors scattered about, they conveniently exclude "poor white" from their dictionary.

racism: *a belief that race is the primary determinant of human traits and capacities and that racial differences produce an inherent superiority of a particular race; racial prejudice or discrimination.—Webster's Ninth New Collegiate Dictionary.*

"I thought racism was when white people hated black people," said LeRoy. Actually, LeRoy is right, but you couldn't tell from the above definition. Neither "black" nor "white" is to be found there.

Just so we all get the correct understanding of this word, the *Oxford English Dictionary*, to its credit, calls it "white racism." It correctly defines this term as the "belief in the superiority of the white race, leading to antagonism towards people of the other races."

It has been said that the white man (more specifically, the racist white man) has made himself an enemy to every other man. Based on the historical record, one would be hard pressed to disprove this claim.

What we call "racism" the *Oxford English Dictionary* calls "racialism." What's "racialism"? It's the "belief in the superiority of a particular race leading to prejudice and antagonism towards people of other races, esp[ecially] those in close proximity who may be felt as a threat to one's cultural and racial integrity or economic well being."

For information on what has been called "Black racism" see "reverse discrimination" discussed below.

redneck: *a white member of the Southern rural laboring class—sometimes used disparagingly.—Webster's Ninth New Collegiate Dictionary.*

The *Oxford English Dictionary* describes "redneck" as "a member of the white rural labouring class of the southern states; one whose attitudes are considered characteristic of this class...Originally, and still often, derogatory, but now also used with more sympathy for the aspirations of the rural American."

"Oh, I get it. Now they want us to feel sorry for the poor white racist redneck," complained one woman of color. So it would seem. But, in all fairness, there are some rural white southerners who aren't "racist rednecks" at all. They are good people who, in some cases, should be sympathized with.

"But what about the poor, disenfranchised blacks who have been victimized by these racist rednecks? Should we have 'sympathy' for their aspirations?" ask the same black woman. In a word: No.

The word "redneck" seems to be synonymous with "poor white" discussed above. (See "poor white" for more information.)

The *American Heritage Dictionary* says that "redneck" is an offensive slang "used as a disparaging term for a member of the white rural laboring class, especially in the southern United States," also "one who is regarded as having a provincial, conservative, often bigoted sociopolitical attitude."

Ultimately, dictionaries ask us to feel sorry for insensitive whites who are often have a "bigoted sociopolitical attitude" toward others, but, though not overtly stated, especially blacks. Is there a derogatory term for a black person that calls for "sympathy" on the part of readers?

(NOTE: What *Webster's Tenth* Says: It expands the definition to read: "a person whose behavior and opinions are similar to those attributed to rednecks—often used disparagingly.")

sambo: *applied in America and Asia to persons of various degrees of mixed Negro and Indian or European blood; also, a name for a kind of yellow monkey.—Oxford English Dictionary.*

This bares repeating: Whenever a person has varying degrees of "Negro" blood in him, powerful white racists come up with an uncomplimentary name for him. That name is often linked to an animal. "Sambo" is the sixth word considered thus far that fractionalizes the black man. (The other five are "Cajun," "Creole," "mulatto," "octoroon," and "quadroon," all considered in Chapter I.)

Webster's Ninth New Collegiate Dictionary simply says the word is "an international style of wrestling employing judo techniques." Unbelievably, they don't say that this is an offensive term for African Americans. Do you remember Sambo's restaurants? This restaurant chain was forced to change its name because of the stigma attached to it.

The news media are particularly guilty of characterizing African American criminals in animalistic terms. "A Predator's Struggle to Tame Himself" was the sensational title of the June 27, 1993 article in the *New York Times* magazine about a black criminal trying to mend his ways.

As if that wasn't enough, the *Oxford English Dictionary* further shows that the word "sambo" is "[a] nickname for a Negro. Now used as a term of abuse....esp[ecially] with reference to the appearance or subservient mentality held to be typical of the black American slave."

The very sight of black people is assailed. This definition suggests an unmotivated, addlewitted, slow-walking, lazy, mentally inept black man. And please note, it says that this is "typical."

The word first occurred in 1748. Its usage in 1833 gives us an idea of the mind set among blacks, whites, Asians, Indians, and others. The following attitude was in print at that time: "A quadroon looks down upon a mulatto, while a mulatto looks down upon a sambo, that is, half mulatto half negro."

A "quadroon," because he is three fourths white and one fourth black, was better than a "mulatto" who was half white and half black. Theoretically, the quadroon would be lighter, hence better. (The definitions for "quadroon" and "mulatto" were considered in Chapter I.)

This shows that "intra-race" racism among black people isn't new. It has been around for as long as the blood of the Black African has been mingled with the blood of other races—but especially the white. So, the more white blood you have in your black body, the better—or, even smarter—you are.

Attesting to this concept are the thoughts of white Berkeley professor Arthur Jensen who believes that light-skinned blacks are more intelligent than dark-skinned ones. According to author Carl Senna in his book *The Fallacy of I.Q.,* Jensen believes that the U.S. government should intervene through eugenics (Hitler-like "master race" breeding) marriage controls.

Jensen isn't alone in his warped view of things. Dr. Fredrick K. Goodwin, director of the Alcohol Drug Abuse and Mental Health Administration (ADAMHA), linked a so-called "violence gene" in black males to male monkeys.

Notice his comments as reported in the book *Don't Believe The Hype:* "If you look, for example, at male monkeys, especially in the wild, roughly half of them survive to adulthood. The other half die by violence.

"That is the natural way of it for males, to knock each other off, and, in fact, there are some interesting evolutionary implications of that because the same hyper-aggressive monkeys who kill each other are also hyper-sexual, so they copulate more....

Maybe it isn't just the careless use of the word when people call certain areas of certain cities 'jungles.'"

Simply put, Goodwin is saying that black men are very violent and often kill one another—just like monkeys. They love having sex and are generally known for their supposed sexual "prowess" and aggressiveness—just like monkeys. It's no wonder then, he concludes, those black neighborhoods in the inner city are called "jungles."

Former Klansman, David Duke, who was unsuccessful in his 1991 bid for the governorship of Louisiana, agrees with Goodwin. He states, according to a March 3, 1992 *Washington Post* article entitled "Scrutinizing David Duke," that African Americans are "more primitive in a lot of ways [and] much more closer to the jungle."

shine: *an abusive term for a Black. Also attrib. U.S. slang—Oxford English Dictionary.*

This word doesn't appear in Webster's dictionaries of the 1990s. Nevertheless, it's uniquely American. Was it really an abusive term? Well, notice how it was used in a book by T. Farrell entitled *Young Manhood III* (1934): "They saw one beautiful blonde girl with a coal-black, sweating nigger, and they said nothing, only because there were too many shines in the place."

The Webster's dictionaries of the 1990s have done well in not including this word as an entry. One has to wonder why they didn't exclude other words that are as blatantly racist as this one.

skinhead: *one whose hair is cut very short, a young short-haired working-class British hoodlum.—Webster's Ninth New Collegiate Dictionary.*

No mention is made at all of this being the member of a violent, racist, white organization that harasses, intimidates, and murders Africans, African Americans, and others.

The *Oxford English Dictionary* says a "skinhead" is "in the U[nited] K[ingdom], a youth (often one of a gang), also typically characterized by wearing workman-like clothing and heavy boots, and by a tendency to aggressive behaviour."

The *American Heritage Dictionary* gives a more robust definition when it describes a "skinhead" as "a member of any of various groups of white British or American youths who shave their heads, gather at rock concerts and sports events, and sometimes participate in white-supremacist and anti-immigrant activities."

Make no mistake about it, the "skinheads" are a violent bunch. In 1973, the British publication *Black Nation* stated: "According to an eye-witness a gang of white skinheads savagely attacked a black youth who today is nearly blind as a result."

(NOTE: What *Webster's Tenth* Says: It adds the more widely known definition: "a usu[ually] white male belonging to any of various sometimes violent youths gangs whose members have close-shaven hair and often espouse white-supremacist beliefs.")

spook: *ghost, specter, an undercover agent; spy. —Webster's Ninth New Collegiate Dictionary.*

Amazingly, there is no indication that this is a derogatory term for the black man. This is a telling omission. Based upon this definition, a white racist can get away with calling a black man a "spook." "After all," he may claim, "the dictionary doesn't say it's a racist name for a black person."

How the editors missed the opportunity to plug the black man into this definition is mystifying since, for the most part, there are a number of negative connotations associated with it.

But, just so we don't lose sight of the real meaning behind this term, the *Oxford English Dictionary* brings things into focus by saying that "spook" is "a derogatory term for a Black person."

In fact, in 1966 a writer for the British publication *New Statesman* said "I find a disturbing minority of my English contemporaries ... pointedly tossing off inconsequential remarks about spades [another offensive name for black men] and spooks in my company."

More recently, in 1977, E. Leonard in the *Unknown Man* said in relief: "We almost had another riot ... The bar-owner ... shoots a spook in the parking lot."

tar baby: *[fr[om] the tar baby which confounded Brer Rabbit in a story in Uncle Remus; His Songs and His Stories (1880) by Joel Chandler Harris] (1926): something from which it is nearly impossible to extricate oneself.—Webster's Ninth New Collegiate Dictionary.*

The term itself signals an ominous origin. You immediately think of a black infant. "Tar" is black and a "baby" is an infant, hence, "black infant." (Compare "pickaninny" discussed earlier in this chapter.)

But, you're right if you say that the above definition doesn't suggest anything of the kind. Keep in mind, though, that the above definition is from perhaps the most racist dictionary in modern history, *Webster's Ninth New Collegiate Dictionary*.

The *Oxford English Dictionary* brings us to reality by telling it like it is. We are told that "tar baby" is "a derog[atory] term for a Black [in the] U.S." Thank you.

(NOTE: What *Webster's Tenth* Says: It neatly kept the status quo. As far as Webster's dictionaries are concerned, "tar baby" isn't an offensive term for a black person. So, if you're feeling feisty and have mustered up enough courage to do so, go ahead and call the next black infant you see a "tar baby." After all, you have the backing of Webster's dictionaries!)

Instead of identifying the Klan as a terrorist organization with a history of murder, rape, torture, etc., the dictionary states that the Klan organization is simply a "fraternal group" of "American-born white Christians." (See "Klu Klux Klan" on page 92.)

The dictionary says only "some states" in the United States observe Martin Luther King's birthday as a legal holiday. In reality it's a federal holiday. (See page 94 under "Martin Luther King Day.") King is shown here with Malcolm X in 1964.

tribe: *a social group comprising numerous families, clans, or generations together with slaves, dependents, or adopted strangers.—Webster's Ninth New Collegiate Dictionary.*

This word offends Africans and those of African heritage. It suggests that which is primitive, backward, archaic, even uncivilized.

Specifically, regarding Africans, the *World Book Encyclopedia* says that "[t]oday, many black Africans and other peoples consider the word *tribe* insulting because they believe it implies that they are primitive. Other so-called tribes consider the term inaccurate because they regard themselves as separate groups.

"For example, the Yoruba, Nigeria's largest ethnic group, is sometimes called a tribe. But they include the Egba, the Ife, the Oyo, and other peoples, each with their own culture and political organization."

Actually, the word "tribe" applied to white peoples first. It literally means, in Latin, "three" ("tri"), "to be" ("bu"). It predates Latin and finds its origin in Greek culture.

"Tribe" was closely associated with how the Greeks divided the population. According to the *Oxford English Dictionary,* "in Greek history the Athenians were divided into four tribes with each tribe being divided into three parts." (Chapter III demonstrates negative Greek attitudes toward black Africans as expressed through various words. "Tribe" could very well be one of those words.)

Aside from these ancient white peoples applying the word "tribe" to segments of their own populations, the modern-day white Irish have their tribes, which they call the "tribes of Galway."

So, the next time you hear the word "tribe," don't just think of the Africans, Australian Aborigines, or the American Indians. Think, first, of the white people who coined the idea and word, and apply it to them—minus, of course, the racist overtone.

Uncle Tom: *[...[a] pious and faithful Negro slave in Uncle Tom's Cabin (1851-52) by Harriet Beecher Stowe.] (1927) a black who is overeager to win the approval of whites.—Websters Ninth New Collegiate Dictionary.*

"Uncle Tom" is a particularly offensive term for a black man. In a way, it's more offensive than "nigger." As *Webster's Tenth* says, one black man can call another black man "nigger," (or "nig-ga," with emphasis on the first syllable) and the second black man wouldn't be offended. This isn't usually the case with "Uncle Tom."

If anyone were to call a black man "Uncle Tom" (whether black or white), he would be extremely offended. Why? Because, unlike the horribly offensive word "nigger," "Uncle Tom" denotes being a traitor to the black race, a "sell out," particularly to the racist white man (or woman). None of this is explained in the above definition.

The *American Heritage Dictionary* at least tells us that it's "offensive." While its definition isn't the fullest, it does describe an "Uncle Tom" as "a Black person who is regarded as being humiliatingly subservient or deferential to white people."

"The person who wrote the definition in both *Webster's Ninth New Collegiate Dictionary* and *Webster's Tenth* obviously wasn't a black man," says Bobby from South Central Los Angeles. "Unless, of course," continues Bobby, "he was an Uncle Tom."

white: *free from color ... of the color of new snow or milk ... of the color white ... lustrous ... being a member of a group or race characterized by reduced pigmentation and usu[ally] specif[ically] distinguished from persons belonging to groups marked by black, brown, yellow, or red skin coloration ... of, relating to, characteristic of, or consisting of white people ... marked by upright fairness ... free from spot or blemish ... free* *from moral impurity : innocent ... marked by the wearing of white by the woman as a symbol of purity ... not intended to cause harm ... favorable, fortunate.—Webster's Ninth New Collegiate Dictionary.*

Is there anything wrong with "white"? Only positive things are stated here. If you take a look at the definition for "black" (discussed earlier in this chapter) in the dictionary, you would be hard pressed to find anything good there.

Let's break down what is stated here by asking a series of questions: If you are "white," are you innately "marked by upright fairness"? If you are "white," are you inherently "free from moral impurity; innocent"? If you are "white," are you intrinsically "favorable, fortunate"?

The answer to these questions is a resounding "Yes!" if you sat on the board of editors for *Webster's Ninth New Collegiate Dictionary*.

Unlike the definition for "black," *Webster's Ninth New Collegiate Dictionary* wants to make it clear that the "white" race is to be clearly "distinguished from persons belonging to groups marked by black, brown, yellow, or red skin coloration."

For further shocking revelations, please compare the complete definition of "white" with the complete definition of "black" (considered earlier in this chapter), and draw your own conclusion. (See also "non-white" in this chapter.)

white backlash: *resentment felt by white people against demands made by, or concessions made to, Black people.—Oxford English Dictionary.*

Is there an expression for the "resentment felt by [black] people against demands made by, or concessions made to, [White] people"? Yes, there is. According to *Webster's Ninth New*

Collegiate Dictionary, the word is "militant." (See "black nationalist" and "Black Panther" in Chapter V.)

Who came up with the expression "white backlash"? Why is it that the English-speaking world is even exposed to such a biased term that seeks to articulate the seemingly justifiable, sympathy-rousing "resentment" felt by whites?

And, oh yes, "Black people" specifically are targets of white "resentment." Curiously, even though some whites feel quite superior to peoples of other non-white races in general (see "white chauvinism" below), "[b]lack people" are singled out (just as they are under the definition of "non-white") as being guilty for causing whites to have "resentment" toward them.

white chauvinism: *orig[inally] U.S., a white person's excessively high regard for his own race.—Oxford English Dictionary.*

Webster's Ninth New Collegiate Dictionary doesn't list this expression. But, by now, we shouldn't be surprised by this omission. If you're like most people, you've heard of "male chauvinism" but didn't know that such an expression as "white chauvinism" was even listed in a dictionary.

Note that "white chauvinism," though closely related, is not quite the same as "white supremacy." The latter is the belief or doctrine that the white race is superior to others—particularly the black race.

white flight: *(1967) the departure of white families usu[ually] from urban neighborhoods undergoing racial integration or from cities implementing school desegregation.—Webster's Ninth New Collegiate Dictionary.*

Well, though this definition is accurate, it's also vague. What races are we talking about when we say "racial integration"? What race is causing white people to flee "urban neighborhoods"?

In answer to these questions, the *Oxford English Dictionary* identifies the offending race. Note how it defines "white flight": "The migration of white people from inner-city areas (esp[ecially] those with large black population) to the suburbs."

Yes, *black* people are causing "white flight." Whether there are good reasons for this situation or not, *Webster's Ninth New Collegiate Dictionary* didn't give it to us straight. It didn't tell us that white people were "flying" away from black people in particular.

This definition, by its very nature, legitimizes white sociological trends. Are there any that legitimizes black ones? If not, why not? And why is it that every time white folks do something or feel a certain way, they get a new dictionary entry for it?

white Negro: *a Negro, or a person of Negro ancestry, who has a pale or albino complexion...a white person who defends the rights and interests of Negroes, or identifies with them.—Oxford English Dictionary.*

Webster's Ninth New Collegiate Dictionary omits this term. It's exclusive to the black-white relationship. That is to say, there's no listing for "white Hispanic" or "white Asian" or "white Indian."

This was meant to offend whites who defended the rights and interests of blacks. It also discouraged well-meaning whites who were inclined to identify themselves with "Negroes."

Why couldn't these whites be called "fair-minded humanitarians"? Why couldn't they be called "good-natured humans with fellow feeling"? Why does the expression "white Negro" even exist?

Since "Negroes" were looked down upon, being a "white Negro" was uncomplimentary. You were still a "Negro," as it were, no matter what adjective preceded the term.

Interestingly, when apartheid was policy in South Africa, visiting black dignitaries weren't treated as were their fellow black indigenous brothers. The black dignitaries were given a lapel badge that read: "Honorable White." Even if he was "black as the ace of spades" he was considered white by the government at the time. He was the ultimate "white Negro."

white nigger: *a derogatory term for a white person who does menial labour,..a Negro who is regarded as deferring to white people or accepting a role prescribed by them.—Oxford English Dictionary.*

You could be black or white and be offended by this term. Through no fault of your own, you could be a conscientious white man working hard at menial labor to make an honest living, and yet risk being called a "white nigger" because of your efforts. Only a sick mind could come up with such awful reasoning.

Of course, if you're black and a hard worker at menial labor, you're a nigger anyway, according to the same racist mind. If you're black and have accepted your lot in life in a dominant white society, you're a "white nigger." Whether you're black or white, under certain circumstances, you could very well be a "white nigger."

white supremacy: *(1867) a doctrine based on a belief in the inherent superiority of the white race over the black race and the correlative necessity for the subordination of blacks to whites in all relationships.—Webster's Ninth New Collegiate Dictionary.*

In plain English, the term "white supremacy" means that some white people believe that all white people are better than all black people, and that the few white people who are in control of things should do everything in their power to make sure that all black people stay below all white people in every way, shape, and form.

The *American Heritage Dictionary* says "white supremacy" is "the belief or theory that the white race is inherently superior to and therefore entitled to rule over all other races."

Are white supremacists groups really alive and well in America? If so, how far-reaching is their influence? Farai Chideya, in her book *Don't Believe The Hype,* offers some staggering statistics in answer to these questions:

"There are several strong white supremacist groups in America, and by some estimates their influence is growing. There are an estimated 250 to 300 white supremacist groups with a total of 10,000 to 30,000 hard-core members. There may be hundreds of thousands of other Americans who support the ideology.

"By some estimates, the number of hate crimes is rising. According to the Southern Poverty Law Center's project Klan Watch, in 1989 there were 7 cross burnings, 24 instances of vandalism, and 125 hate-crime related murders. By 1992, those numbers had risen to 31 cross burnings, 117 instances of vandalism, and 322 murders.

"And in 1991, the FBI counted a total of over 4,500 hate crimes in the United States....California is headquarters to the largest white supremacist group in the nation. The group White Aryan Resistance (WAR) is headed by Tom Metzger, a former Ku Klux Klan leader who lives in [Fallbrook] San Diego County."

What are we to conclude? This: When white supremacists, who believe that whites are superior to blacks, employ strategies to suppress and oppress blacks "in all relationships," and blacks, who long for a country or nation where they can be free of the tyranny of the dominant white culture, respond by simply desiring such, they are called "militant." What a frightful mislabeling.

wog: *[prob[ably] short for golliwog]...(ca. 1934): a dark-skinned foreigner...one from the Middle East or Far*

East—usu[ally] used disparagingly.—Webster's Ninth New Collegiate Dictionary.

The British came up with the word "wog" which is short for "golliwog" (discussed earlier in this chapter), a grossly offensive word for a black man.

To demonstrate that the word "wog" is associated with the black man, a publication entitled *Essay On Oxford,* written in 1932 by J.P. Hewison, says: "And here the Ethiop[ian] ranks, the wogs."

Admittedly, the word appears primarily to be applied to Arabs. The *American Heritage Dictionary* says that it's "chiefly british & offensive slang" that's "used as a disparaging term for a person of color, especially a foreigner from the Middle East or Asia."

The *American Heritage Dictionary* also goes on to say that "wog" is "probably short for golliwog." The *Oxford English Dictionary* describes "wog" as "a vulgarly offensive name for a foreigner, esp. one of Arab extraction." Though it isn't stated here, another slang term identifying dark-skinned Arabs with American blacks is "sand niggers."

woolly-headed: *having hair suggesting wool; marked by vague or confused perception or thinking.—Webster's Ninth New Collegiate Dictionary.*

Now, who do you suppose they could be referring to here? Who is it that has "hair suggesting wool" and is perceived as being dull-witted? Well, it isn't Forest Gump with an Afro. It's the black man.

Is this an overreaction? Definitely not. The *Oxford English Dictionary* plainly states that a "woolly-head" is "a person with wooly hair, esp[ecially] (disparagingly) a Black, a Negro."

III. The Greek Origin of Racist Words

"Do not give your heart to all the words that people may speak."
—Ecclesiastes 7:21, *New World Translation*

αβγ

Don't listen to everything the dictionary tells you! Linguists and lexicographers agree that dictionaries, like the people who write them, have biases. Some of these biases go as far back as the ancient Greeks. In fact, the words tell a story themselves. See if you can find the story in the following words:

Andromeda [Greek, ανδρομεδα]: *a mythological Ethiopian princess rescued from a monster by her future husband Perseus.—Webster's Ninth New Collegiate Dictionary.*

Although Andromeda was depicted as a black African here, Hollywood turned her white. That's the first thing wrong. Secondly, in this account of interracial marriage—ancient Greek style—whites and blacks alike see a helpless, outstandingly beautiful black woman (of some means and stature) being rescued by a white man. How quaint.

Andromeda was so beautiful that Poseidon (the Greek god of the sea) "sent a sea monster that could only be appeased by her sacrifice," according to the 1991 *Concise Columbia Encyclopedia* (CCE).

According to Dr. Shelley Haley, a classical professor at Hamilton College, Greeks were so infatuated with African women that "the Greeks took Egyptian and Ethiopian women as mistresses." Apparently, the only way a Greek man would enter into honorable marriage with an Egyptian or Ethiopian woman was in a myth.

The enthralling effect these black women had on Greek men is reflected in a poem written by the ancient Greek writer Asclepiades.

Of a beautiful African woman named Didyme, he wrote: "When I gaze at her beauty I melt like wax before a fire; if she is dark, what of it? So are coals." Despite this woman being black as coals, she was viewed as having fiery beauty.

That a white man would say such a thing about a black woman is not restricted to the mythology of ancient Greek culture. Like Perseus and Andromeda, today, white men marry beautiful black women.

Modern-day society doesn't seem too disturbed when this happens. But, the questions are: How do some whites react when the shoe is on the other foot? What do they say when a black man hooks up with a beautiful white woman?

Author T. Farrell, in his book *Young Manhood III* (1934), details the feeling of certain whites. He writes: "They saw one beautiful blonde girl with a coal-black, sweating nigger, and they said nothing, only because there were too many [niggers] in the place."

As if history took notes to expose a double standard, the "coal-black" man in this scene is called a "sweating nigger" because he is with a beautiful blonde white female. When a beautiful African woman, dark as "coals" is with a white man, it's considered beautiful ancient poetry. This unfortunate reality is consistent with what history tell us.

In short, history discloses to us, as is briefly demonstrated in this chapter, that the Greeks have denigrated attractive and unattractive African women, particularly those of Egyptian and Ethiopian origin.

So, women of color, just think: in order to have made your way into a wonderful Greek story, myth, or fairytale, you had to have had money, beauty, and royal blood flowing through your veins.

callipygian [Greek, καλλίπῦγος]: *having shapely buttocks.—Webster's Ninth New Collegiate Dictionary.*

"What could possibly be wrong with this word?" you may be asking yourself. Well, plenty.

First of all, it's a Greek word. That immediately gives us a hint that there may be an underlying racist theme. Upon closer examination, unfortunately, we aren't disappointed.

What's implied here is that "having shapely buttocks" is something more or less exclusively white—or at least not black. We can see this by examining another Greek word that describes the buttocks.

The word is one that most of us have never heard of. It's "steatopygia"—a medical term. Now *Webster's Ninth New Collegiate Dictionary* defines this word as having "an excessive development of fat on the buttocks esp[ecially] of females that is common among the Hottentots and some Negro peoples."

Yes, African women and women from other "Negro peoples" have "an excessive development of fat on the buttocks." Have you ever seen white women (and women of other races) with fat buttocks? According to *Webster's Ninth New Collegiate Dictionary*, if you have, it's not a medical condition. Or, if you have, they don't have a word for it. Remember, both "callipygian" and "steatopygia" are Greek words.

The denigration of the black woman by the Greeks and expounded on by the European powers is both egregious and offensive. They say the gorilla is named after one "tribe" ("ethnic group" is the more acceptable term) of African women (see below), and, now, another "tribe" (the Hottentots), is flawed with excessive fat on their back sides!

The *Oxford English Dictionary* defines "callipygian" this way: "Of, pertaining to, or having well-shaped or finely developed buttocks." (See the word "steatopygia" below for more information.)

So, if you're an African or an African-American woman, you don't have to sit on your buttocks, whether they have excessive fat or not, and take this. Be proud, and don't allow your beauty to be defined by white racists.

Ethiopian [Greek, Αἰθιοψ]: *a member of any of the mythical or actual peoples usu[ally] described by the ancient Greeks as dark-skinned and living far to the south; Negro.—Webster's Ninth New Collegiate Dictionary.*

The black Ethiopians are described through the eyes of a white, hostile foreign power—the ancient Greeks. Immediately we are introduced to this African culture by a people who looked down on them. Does *Webster's Ninth New Collegiate Dictionary* define any European nation through the eyes of an ancient Black African nation? Absolutely not.

The Greeks were so into myths that they made the Ethiopians a "mythical...dark-skinned" people. Why "mythical"? They are as real today as they were back then. And the various ethnic groups of modern-day Ethiopia are just as "dark-skinned." In fact, the term "Ethiopia" apparently means "Region of (Sun) Burnt Faces." If it means this, then it's an offensive term.

Burnt items are unsightly. Therefore, calling the faces of these Africans "burnt" is an insult. If they must be distinguished, calling them "dark" is much more acceptable. Interestingly, there are several ancient Greek words for "dark." Why wasn't one of these used? Apparently, it's because the word "Ethiopian" was meant to be derogatory!

How did the Ethiopian's skin turn black? Mary Lefkowitz, in her book, *NOT Out of Africa,* asks: Could it be "that the Ethiopians' skin turned black when Phaethon borrowed his father the Sun God's chariot, and brought it too near the earth?"

This is precisely what one ancient Greek writer alleged. The Ethiopians were black as a result of some freak accident on the part of the Sun God's son hot-rodding around the solar system in Daddy's chariot. That's Greek mythology for you.

While on the subject of Greek tales and mythology, the name of the fable-telling Aesop, who was black according to scholars, is of interest. Though not an authority on the subject, the well-read Malcolm X, in his autobiography, said that "'Aesop' was the only Greek name for an Ethiopian." This isn't hard for some to believe since "Ethiopian" and "Aesop" are apparently related in Greek.

According to this definition, the word is made fun of and considered contemptuous. In view of the preponderance of evidence considered thus far, the ancient Greeks were making fun of these North Africans when *they* named them "Ethiopians."

gorilla [Greek, γοριλλα]: *(1853) believed to be the name of an alleged African tribe of hairy women.—Webster's Ninth New Collegiate Dictionary.*

Unbelievable. Shocking. Bewildering. The ancient Greeks have struck again! "Gorilla" is indeed, a Greek word. A more detailed history of this word is worth our investigation. For starters, the *Concise Columbia Encyclopedia* says gorillas were "a tribe of hairy women, perhaps of African origin."

This word eventually took on a scientific flavor thanks to a white American, Dr. Thomas S. Savage. He used the Greek classics and Greek literature to link the gorilla with black women. This scientific influence lends a type of pseudo validation to the thought that gorillas and black women are somehow scientifically connected.

For those of you who may have noticed that the word "alleged" is used (as in "an *alleged* African tribe of hairy women"), be advised that it didn't appear in the definition of an earlier version. In the 1973 version of *Webster's New Collegiate Dictionary* the definition of "gorilla" reads: "An African tribe of hairy women."

The *Oxford English Dictionary* makes sure we don't confine our understanding of the word "gorilla" to primarily black women. It adds: "A person who resembles a gorilla." Since gorillas are black, could they possibly mean a big black man? (One dictionary says the "gorilla" came from "a tribe of hairy black men"!)

What's really being said here is, "we're not just talking about your mother, your sister, your aunt, your female cousin, your wife, your sister-in-law, your daughter, and your daughter-in-law, we're calling you a 'gorilla' too, black man." This definition, as it is, is both brutal and monstrous.

Demonstrating that this isn't just an emotional overreaction, in September 1993, American telecommunications giant AT&T printed an offensive cartoon in its employees' magazine, *Focus*. It depicted a caller on each continent of the earth—all human, except for Africa, which had (as you may have guessed by now) a gorilla standing on it.

The Washington Post, in its September 17, 1993 issue, carried an apology for AT&T in the form of an article entitled, "AT&T Apologizes for Racist Illustration." However, the fact that the *Focus* article appeared in the first place is a sad commentary on the insensitive nature of even "responsible" corporate giants in American society.

(NOTE: What *Webster's Tenth* Says: Its even more insulting than the Ninth edition. It defines "gorilla" as "a tribe of hairy women mentioned in an account of a voyage around Africa.")

Ku Klux Klan: *a post-Civil War secret society advocating white supremacy; a 20th century secret fraternal group held to confine its membership to American-born white Christians. —Webster's Ninth New Collegiate Dictionary.*

This expression is from a Greek word that means "circle" (kuklos, κυκλος). Examples of this word are found in the "New Testament" at Mark 3:34, Revelation 4:6; 5:11 and 7:11. Since the Klan identify themselves as "Christians," they apparently use (or *mis*use) the Bible to support their outlandish beliefs. (For more information on the Klan, see Chapters V and VI.)

Memnon [Greek, μεμνον]: *an Ethiopian king slain by Achilles at a late stage of the Trojan War.—Webster's Ninth New Collegiate Dictionary.*

Sources disagree as to whether the mythological Memnon was a black Ethiopian king, or a white king over Ethiopia. One source says he was "the son of the Trojan prince Tithonus and of Eos, goddess of the dawn." (Microsoft *Encarta.*)

Judging from the above definition, Webster's editors apparently think he's black. If he was, we have a white man who killed a black man in war. Okay. Fine. War is war. War is hell. You either kill or be killed.

But, what these editors left out was the happy ending the black King Memnon experienced. Not to worry. The *American Heritage Dictionary* inserted it. It says Memnon, in Greek mythology, was "[a]n Ethiopian king killed by Achilles and made immortal by Zeus."

This was a generous act on the part of Zeus. The ancient Greeks were not always so kind to the Ethiopians. At times they associated them with animals. (See "gorilla" in Chapter III.)

For instance, in her book *Not Out of Africa,* Dr. Mary Lefkowitz, a critic of Afrocentric thought, mentions a fourth-century B.C. vase that depicted the faces of an Ethiopian and a satyr (a mythical creature with the body of a man but with pointed ears, a horse's tail and goat's legs). Ironically, this is inconsistent with Zeus granting Memnon immortality.

This illustrates a weird sort of respectful loathing the ancient Greeks had for Ethiopians. Interestingly, during the days of slavery, some black people believed that slaves killed by their masters were "made immortal," like Memnon, "by [God]."

steatopygia [Greek, στεατοπυγια]: *an excessive development of fat on the buttocks esp[ecially] of females that is common among the Hottentots and some Negro peoples.—Webster's Ninth New Collegiate Dictionary.*

Black women everywhere have fat butts! That's what this definition is saying. Just look at five words in it and you'll no doubt readily see the subliminal, racist slant. The words, in order, are: "excessive," "fat," "buttocks," "females," "Negro." Other dictionaries are just as damning in their definitions.

The *Oxford English Dictionary* is a culprit in perpetrating the racist fraud. It states that "steatopygia" is "a protuberance of the buttocks due to an abnormal accumulation of fat in and behind the hips and thighs, found (more markedly in women than in men) as a racial characteristic of certain peoples, esp[ecially] the Hottentots and Bushmen of South Africa."

The *American Heritage Dictionary*, thankfully, doesn't implicate the black woman at all. It simply states that "steatopygia" is "an extreme accumulation of fat on the buttocks."

The covert, subtle suggestion inherent in the word "steatopygia" is that, once again, the standard for "regular-shaped" buttocks, particularly for females, is the white woman. In fact, there's a word for a pair of "regular-shaped," beautiful buttocks that imply that they belong to a white woman. The word is "callipygous." (See "callipygian" above.)

Suffice it to say that many ethnic groups have distinguishing physical characteristics which are not denigrated in a biased term.

"They're just angry that they don't have what I have," said Jackie, a rather vocal, noticeably callipygous black woman. "If they don't like it, they can just kiss my big black callipygous ass!" Aside from acknowledging Jackie's frustration, the author has no comment.

IV. Racist Words: Science and Medicine

"The simple man believes every word he hears;
a clever man understands the need for proof."
—Proverbs 14:15, *The New English Bible*

You just cannot believe every word you read in the dictionary, even when these words are spoken in the hallowed names of science and medicine. In a surprising amount of instances, there's little or no proof to the claims scientists make about the supposed physical defects or imperfections of black people.

cystic fibrosis: *a common hereditary disease esp[ecially] among whites that appears usu[ally] in early childhood.—Webster's Ninth New Collegiate Dictionary.*

While all disease is bad, in plain English, this is a disease that white people get. What sickle-cell anemia is to blacks (in the minds of most, even blacks), cystic fibrosis is to whites. But, not all reputable, well-known dictionaries will tell you that.

The *American Heritage Dictionary* doesn't mention at all that white people—NOT BLACK PEOPLE—get this disease. The *Concise Columbia Encyclopedia* doesn't mention it either. If you check other important reference works, they are silent on the matter.

"But, shouldn't Webster's be given credit for saying it like it is?" Yes and No.

Yes, they stated things frankly in the Ninth and Tenth editions. But, just when you think things are too good to be true, they usually are.

In the recent 1994 paperback edition, Webster defines cystic fibrosis as "a common hereditary disease marked esp[ecially] by deficiency of pancreatic enzymes, by respiratory symptoms, and by excessive loss of salt in the sweat." THEY MAKE NO MENTION THAT it's THE WHITE MAN'S DISEASE!

This omission is curious—and offensive—in contrast to their treatment of sickle-cell anemia which, they say, "occurs esp[ecially] in individuals of African...ancestry" in the very same 1994 paperback edition.

melanin: *a dark brown or black animal or plant pigment.—Webster's Ninth New Collegiate Dictionary.*

Though this word may not be racist in and of itself, it's an ancient Greek word. That alone makes it suspect. The Greek word for "black" or "dark" is "melan-" (Greek, μελαν-). In combination with another English word, the racist nature of "melan-" becomes clearly discernible.

The word in question is "melancholia." It means, according to *Webster's Ninth New Collegiate Dictionary*, "a mental condition characterized by extreme depression, bodily complaints, and often hallucinations and delusions; esp[ecially] a manic-depressive psychosis."

Now, "melanin" could also mean "dark brown or black" skin. "Melancholia" basically means deep, "extreme depression." This prompts the question: Is a subtle connection being made here between "dark" skin and negative mental states? (Incidentally, yet another negative word for a black man is "darky.")

And what about "melanoma"? It's described as "a usu[ally] malignant tumor containing dark pigment," or, in other words, skin cancer. That's ironic. The skin of black people contains dark pigment, yet white people, unfortunately, are more susceptible to skin cancer. It's interesting, and disturbing, to see the racist linguistic connections the ancient Greeks made: dark skin, psychosis, cancer, etc.

nude: *the color of Caucasian flesh.—Webster's Ninth New Collegiate Dictionary.*

How arrogant! First of all, *Webster's Ninth New Collegiate Dictionary* is the only major dictionary (to the author's best knowledge) that has this definition.

It subtly suggests that the natural, beautiful color of human skin, is white. With all of the beautiful colors, hues, and tones of human flesh (including the bronzed beauty of tanned white flesh!), we are lead to believe that the raw, white flesh of the Caucasian is representative flesh of humans when they are unclothed.

To their credit, the editors of *The Merriam Webster Dictionary* (1994) give a more acceptable definition of the word "nude": "A nude human figure...the condition of being nude." Happily, they didn't say "a nude *white* human figure."

(NOTE: What *Webster's Tenth* Says: It rewords the definition to read: "The color of a white person's flesh." Let's not bite our tongue. They've jumped from the frying pan into the fire with this definition! What's the name of the color of a black person's flesh?)

phylogeny: *racial history of a kind of organism.—Webster's Ninth New Collegiate Dictionary.*

"Phylogeny" is suspected as being used, scientifically, to determine what fraction of black blood is found in a white person. Since this is done under the auspices of science, it gives the distinct impression of validity and legitimacy.

Webster's Ninth New Collegiate Dictionary falls distressingly short when it excludes that "phylogeny" is employed to support the belief systems of confused, bewildered, miserable racists, or, more simply, that it is used to determine the blood composition of humans—racially speaking.

On the other hand, the *Oxford English Dictionary* is, ostensibly, more honest. It describes "phylogeny" as "the genesis and evolution of the phylum, tribe, or species; ancestral or racial evolution of an animal or plant type...as distinguished from ontogenesis, the evolution of the individual."

The word first appeared in print in Darwin's *Origin of the Species* (1872) It's a word derived from the ancient Greek words *phylon* (φυλον, *race*) and *geneia* (γενεια, *origin*). Historical evidence, some of which have been considered here, strongly suggests that Darwin and the ancient Greeks were racists. (Compare "eugenics," though not considered in this work, in your copy of the dictionary. See "sambo" in Chapter II for a brief discussion of it.)

(NOTE: What *Webster's Tenth* Says: It changes the definition by replacing "racial" with "evolutionary." Why the change? You'll have to ask the editors.)

sickle-cell anemia: *a chronic inherited anemia in which a large proportion or the majority of the red blood cells tend to sickle, which occurs primarily in individuals of Negro ancestry.—Webster's Ninth New Collegiate Dictionary.*

This dreadful disease doesn't primarily occur in blacks! We've all been deceived, and, once again, the black man has gotten the short end of the stick.

While it's true that medical science isn't an exact science, that's no reason to misstate the facts.

In a front page article dealing with sickle-cell anemia, the *Los Angeles Times,* January 31, 1995, had this to say concerning the origins of the disease: "Sickle cell anemia is an inherited disease that is most common among people whose ancestors came from Africa, the Middle East, the Mediterranean basin and India."

The World Health Organization says that worldwide, 250,000 babies are born every year with sickle cell anemia. It's estimated that about 72,000 blacks have the disease in the U.S. This is an infinitesimally small amount when you consider that there are 30 million blacks in the U.S.

It shouldn't be surprising, therefore, to find that most people in the U.S. suffering from sickle cell anemia ARE NOT BLACK! Yet, it's called a "black" disease!

Dorland's Illustrated Medical Dictionary—Twenty-fifth Edition displays a slight hint of bias when it says that the disease occurs "almost exclusively in Negroes."

The *American Heritage Dictionary* uses similar wording in describing the disease. It says sickle-cell anemia occurs "almost exclusively in Black people of Africa or of African descent."

The *Concise Columbia Encyclopedia* is just as telling, but, to its credit, it includes others who have sickle-cell anemia. It states that sickle cell anemia is an "inherited disorder occurring mainly among Africans and people of African descent but also among people from the Mediterranean and India."

The *Oxford English Dictionary* indicts Africa too when it describes sickle cell anemia as "[o]ne of the characteristic crescent-shaped red cells found in the blood of people with sickle cell aneamia...occurring in individuals...an autosomal gene found in man...which is especially common in tropical Africa."

A publication called *Listner* (November 26, 1959 issue) says that "sickle cell trait can be found in parts of Africa, in some

Since a very rich, beautiful black African princess was mentioned in Greek mythology, the ancient Greeks made sure a white hero got her. (See "Andromeda" on page 65.)

Dictionaries compare this mule with a "mixed race" black and white baby called a "mulatto." (See "mulatto" on page 8.)

Mediterranean countries, and in parts of India." In fact, according to *The People's Chronology,* what came to be known as "sickle cell anemia" was first discovered in someone other than an African or African American.

"Chicago physician James Bryan Herrick, 49, examines a West Indian student of 20 and makes the first diagnosis of sickle cell anemia," says the above publication. "It will be given the name in 1922."

So, it appears that persons from India, Turkey, Italy, Greece, and other Mediterranean Sea countries (including four countries of Northern Africa), are susceptible to sickle cell anemia. But, let *Webster's Tenth* tell you, mainly Africans and African Americans have this disease. (See "thalassemia" below.)

(NOTE: What *Webster's Tenth* Says: It gives a fuller definition which states that sickle-cell anemia "occurs primarily in individuals of African, Mediterranean, or southwest Asian ancestry." You have to wonder why they didn't add these words in the first place. Instead, the Ninth edition leads you to believe that, as it says, it "occurs primarily in individuals of Negro ancestry.")

Tay Sachs disease: *a fatal hereditary disorder of lipid metabolism characterized by the accumulation of lipids esp[ecially] in nervous tissue due to an enzyme deficiency.—Webster's Ninth New Collegiate Dictionary.*

Let's come straight to the point. "Tay Sachs disease" is primarily a disease afflicting Jewish children from Eastern Europe. This is a tragedy in and of itself. But, why not tell the simple truth that this is a "Jewish" disease?

Webster's Ninth New Collegiate Dictionary was quick to tell us, erroneously, that "sickle-cell anemia" is mostly a "Negro" disease. Why not give a full disclosure of the truth regarding "Tay Sachs disease"?

Webster's Ninth New Collegiate Dictionary anxiously informs us that Jews are associated with other words that start with the letter "t" such as "tallith," "tefillin," "territorialism," and "Torah." Again, why not "Tay Sachs disease"? What proof, if any, is there that "Tay Sachs disease" is a Jewish one?

Well, we can't really look to the *Oxford English Dictionary* for evidence in this regard, even though it gives us the history of the men it was named after.

Of course, Dr. Warren Tay was British, so, his name comes first in "Tay Sachs disease." Dr. Bernard Sachs was an American. His name comes second in this dual Anglo-American medical team. Uncharacteristically, even the Jews were slighted here by having "their" horrible disease named after *goyim* (non-Jews).

The *Oxford English Dictionary* tells us: "The names of Warren Tay (1843-1927), British ophthalmologist, and Bernard Sachs (1858-1944), American physician and neurologist, [are] used...with reference to a fatal inherited...disorder...resulting in idiocy and death in childhood."

There's no hint that this disease is, for all intents and purposes, a Jewish one. But, as was mentioned, they are sure to identify the white nationalities (Anglo and American) of the men whose names label the disease. And, of course, although they don't tell you of the Jewish link to the disease, in the blink of an eye, they'll charge the entire "Negro" race with a disease that only a relative few may have.

But, despite yet another "sin of omission" on the part of the editors of *Webster's Ninth New Collegiate Dictionary*, under the heading of "idiocy," *Dorland's Illustrated Medical Dictionary —Twenty-fifth Edition* says "Tay Sachs disease" chiefly effects "children of Jewish ancestry."

The *American Heritage Dictionary* honestly tells us that it's "a hereditary disease that affects young children almost exclusively of eastern European Jewish descent....resulting in mental retardation, convulsions, blindness, and, ultimately, death."

Finally the *Concise Columbia Encyclopedia* confesses that "Tay Sachs disease" is a "[r]are hereditary disease of infants, ... [that] occurs almost exclusively among Jews of Eastern European descent."

You'd think, with all these references, the Merriam-Webster people would get a clue and reveal to the world the connection between Jews and "Tay Sachs disease" in their latest (as of this writing) edition. If you're thinking this, you're wrong.

Amazingly, even though it's a given in medical science, the Merriam Webster Dictionary, 1994 edition, still doesn't admit that this disease primarily occurs among eastern European Jews.

It says, without mentioning Jews at all, that "Tay Sachs disease" is "[a] hereditary disorder caused by the absence of an enzyme needed to break down fatty material, marked by build-up of lipids in nervous tissue, and causing death in childhood."

One of the things that makes this conspiracy of silence so difficult to stick is that someone forgot to hide the May 8, 1975 issue of *Nature* magazine. It reveals a fact not well known to people who live outside of Israel.

With brutal honesty, it says that "Israel's best known ethnic malady is Tay-Sachs Disease, a fatal genetic disorder limited almost entirely to infants whose forebears came here from certain parts of East Europe."

It isn't only a sad commentary on the literary world, the greater sadness is found in the disease itself, and that innocent Jewish children are stricken with it.

(NOTE: What *Webster's Tenth* Says: It expands the definition by saying that it's "[a] hereditary disorder of lipid metabolism typically affecting individuals of eastern European Jewish ancestry." This is an improvement. But why, as mentioned above, did the editors negate this good move by not identifying the Eastern European Jewish ancestry in the more recent 1994 pocket sized edition!?)

thalassemia (Greek, θᾴλασσεμια): a disease that "*occurs with relatively high frequency in Negro, Mediterranean, or Oriental populations."—Webster's Ninth New Collegiate Dictionary.*

For the most part, *Webster's Ninth New Collegiate Dictionary* has been subtle with its racist propaganda. However, in this definition, we find an outright lie! "Thalassemia" occurs very infrequently, if ever, in black people. *Webster's Ninth New Collegiate Dictionary* itself says, under another entry, that thalassemia major "occurs esp[ecially] in children of Mediterranean parents." (See "Cooley's anemia" in *Webster's Ninth New Collegiate Dictionary*.)

The *American Heritage Dictionary* admits that it's "an inherited form of anemia occurring chiefly among people of Mediterranean descent." Black people, rightly so, aren't even mentioned.

In 1932, a team of researchers (Whipple & Bradford) said, in part, with reference to populations most affected with the disease: "The disease is limited almost wholly to Italians, Greeks, [Turks], and Syrians, i.e., to the people originating about the Mediterranean Sea. For this reason the term 'thalassemia' [from the Greek θᾴλασσα, which means "sea," as in Mediterranean Sea]...may have an appeal."

What! Italians, Greeks, Turks, and Syrians, but no "Negroes"? Happily, *Webster's Tenth* corrected the problem. Well, did they really? (See following "NOTE.")

(NOTE: What *Webster's Tenth* Says: It expands and corrects, to a certain extent, the definition by saying it "occur[s] esp[ecially] in individuals of Mediterranean, black, or southeast Asian ancestry."

Actually, although "Negro" has been relegated to a secondary status in the list of afflicted peoples and replaced with "black," it probably shouldn't be in the list at all. Why? Because, relatively speaking, according to informal interviews conducted with medical personnel, you can count on both hands (and maybe one foot) how many "black" people have "thalassemia." This is a far cry from it occurring "with relatively high frequency in Negro ... populations," according to *Webster's Ninth New Collegiate Dictionary*. In fact, no other major dictionary, medical or otherwise, lists "Negroes" or "blacks" as a people who is susceptible to thalassemia. To the editors of Webster's dictionaries we say: "If you're going to fix it, fix it right.")

white death: *a name for tuberculosis....specially a disease of white men.*—The *Oxford English Dictionary*.

Webster's Ninth New Collegiate Dictionary doesn't list this term at all. The reason is obvious, namely, the words: "specially a disease for white men." Why, this is the equivalent of what *Webster's Ninth New Collegiate Dictionary* would have us believe about black men and sickle cell anemia. While we are told that sickle cell anemia is a "black" or "Negro" disease, in reality, it's not. (See "sickle-cell anemia.")

The expression "white death" casts, in the minds of white racists, a negative light on the supposed superior white race. But, that isn't all.

Although *Webster's Ninth New Collegiate Dictionary* doesn't list the expression "white death," it lists the expression "black death." It defines "black death" as being from "the black patches formed on the skin of its victims" in "a severe epidemic of plague that occurred in Asia and Europe in the 14th century." True, the "black" part of "black death" is describing dark patches on the skin of white people, not blacks. Even so, a sick racist mind (and even uninitiated innocents) could very well associate the "black" part of "black death" to black people.

V. Politics, The Law, and Racism

"A soft answer turns away wrath,
but harsh words cause quarrels."
—Proverbs 15:1, *Living Bible*

There's a lot of quarreling in political circles. Few, though, are as debilitating as political prejudice as expressed in dictionary words. Some black political organizations are victimized by how they are defined by the white establishment. After the quarreling is over, African-Americans are left with something far worst than a "black eye."

Looking through racist lenses, the black man has a distorted view of himself. Not only are "harsh words" about the black man found in the dictionary, they're also in the white man's law books. But, you won't need a lawyer to figure these words out. The fine print is **bold**!

black nationalist: *(1964): a member of a group of militant blacks who advocate separatism from the whites and the formations of self-governing black communities.—Webster's Ninth New Collegiate Dictionary.*

Did you notice the word "militant"? This word isn't used at all in *Webster's Ninth New Collegiate Dictionary* for groups like the Ku Klux Klan, neo-Nazis, and skinheads. In fact, it doesn't even give us a hint that these groups are violent!

Despite this prejudice, it's common knowledge that these white supremacists are known for their violent, murderous actions against blacks, Jews, and others. Some white supremacist organizations have their own "militia"!

There are so many things wrong with the general white perception of "black nationalism" that the subject is too convoluted and complex to be treated fairly in the short space allotted here. We will, nonetheless, try to do a lot with a little.

A more accurate definition of "black nationalist" would be "a black person who advocates separatism from a white, racist society that has designed mechanisms to discriminate against and otherwise oppress the black man."

Separatist movements by black leaders like Paul Cuffe, Martin R. Delany, and Marcus Garvey have historically been, no, not militant, but peaceful. But even peaceful means didn't always work.

When a peaceful black African ship captain named Alfred C. Sam sailed about 60 African Americans back to Africa in 1915, British officials maneuvered to have his ship confiscated. Neither Sam nor any of the men mentioned above was "militant" in his actions. These black men were practicing nonviolence long before Dr. Martin Luther King made it popular.

So, black man, in the same spirit of nonviolence, if you happen to be walking down the street at night in a predominantly white neighborhood and you see an angry group of white supremacists coming toward you, don't worry! Just open up *Webster's Ninth New Collegiate Dictionary* and show them where they aren't described as being "militant"!

black panther: *(1965) a member of an organization of militant American Blacks.—Webster's Ninth New Collegiate Dictonary.*

There are three things wrong with this definition. First, the word "militant" is used! (See above definition.) Whenever too many black men get together, suspicious white forces within our society call them, or their organization, "militant."

This attitude goes back to the days of slavery when, under certain circumstances, it was "against the law" for blacks to congregate for fear of a slave revolt. Some whites fear black retribution in the form of a political revolution. (See "holler" in Chapter VII.)

Second, this definition is in the present tense, but, the Black Panther Party that was started in 1965 as indicated in the definition no longer exists. The definition, written as it is, promotes fear and mistrust of blacks in general, and gives the distinct impression that the Black Panther Party should be feared NOW.

By way of contrast, the Chinese "tong" organization still exists today, but, according to *Webster's Ninth New Collegiate Dictionary*, it was *"formerly* notorious for gang warfare." (See "tong" below.) Though Webster's dictionaries are occasionally unkind to other races, they specifically target the black race.

Third, the definition doesn't give the whole story as to why the Black Panther Party found it necessary to be, as the editors call it, "militant." The complete name of the political party was The Black Panther Party for Self-Defense. They found it necessary to "defend" themselves from white law enforcement officers who brutalized them, as well as other black men.

The 1993 Microsoft *Encarta* Multimedia Encyclopedia describes the Black Panther Party as "originally a kind of community action club for the self-defense of black people." The Black Panther Party was "originally" NOT a "militant" group. Neither were they black racists.

In his book *Long Time Gone* (1996), former Black Panther William Lee Brent, who hijacked a plane to Cuba some twenty-five years ago, wrote: "Panther chairman Bobby Seale stressed the nonracist character of the Black Panther Party. He said the Panthers would work with anyone who was serious about fighting to end racism, social and political injustice, and police brutality."

Some whites were so comfortable with the Panthers that, according to Brent, "all kinds of people hung around the Panther office—members and nonmembers. Whites, especially antiwar and antiracist activists, were constantly coming in to make contributions of money and office supplies....They and the Panthers got along well."

The Panthers even listened to and played white music by the likes of Bob Dylan and the Righteous Brothers at the Oakland headquarters. This so-called vicious, militant, racist black group was so comfortable around whites that some members of their leadership were **married** to white women, even as Brent himself was.

Because the Panthers were not anti-white, other black liberation groups distrusted them. "The most important thing I learned from the trip [to New York]," Brent confesses, "was that the black liberation movement had serious problems of disunity, especially around the Panthers and their policy of coalition with whites."

Despite these facts, the "militant" Panthers were, according to the FBI's first director, J. Edgar Hoover, "the most dangerous group of militants in the country."

Of course, he never said that about the Ku Klux Klan, who are described as "Christians" in *Webster's Ninth New Collegiate Dictionary*! (See definition below.) The implications make for some interesting scenarios.

For instance, if you are a recent immigrant to the U.S. who is learning English, and you read both definitions ("Black Panther" and "Ku Klux Klan") in *Webster's Ninth New Collegiate Dictionary*, you would no doubt be terrified of a member of the "militant" Black

Panther Party, but would feel right at home, at ease with a serene, Christ-like, brotherly, white American "Christian" who is a Klansman. God help you if you do.

To be sure, the Black Panther Party was a "militant" organization as is the Klan. But, asking a few questions will put things into perspective. How many white people did members of the Black Panther Party kill? How many black people has the Klan killed?

The Black Panther Party was born in the 1960s and essentially died (or was killed by the government) in the early 1970s. The Klan was born in the 1860s and is a living, thriving organization (with no signs of dying) in the mid-1990s. Why do you suppose that is?

contraband: *a Negro slave who during the Civil War escaped to or was brought within Union lines.—Webster's Ninth New Collegiate Dictionary.*

The *Oxford English Dictionary* says the word "contraband" was "[u]sed during the American Civil War for: a negro slave... esp[ecially] a fugitive or captured slave; from a decision of Gen. Butler in 1861 that such slaves were contraband of war."

Applying this term to humans was unspeakable. As noted above, General Benjamin Franklin Butler decided that "fugitive or captured" black slaves were contraband.

No wonder he was dismissed as military governor of New Orleans. His arbitrary rule was so harsh and inhumane that he was called "Beast Butler." "And they said the 'Negro' was a beast," quipped one justifiably disgruntled black man. (See also "maroon" in Chapter VII.)

grandfather clause: *a provision in several southern state constitutions designed to enfranchise poor whites and disfranchise Negroes by waiving high voting requirements for descendants of* *men voting before 1867.—Webster's Ninth New Collegiate Dictionary.*

The honesty of this definition is brutal. No matter how free, prosperous, and educated the black man could be, the intent of the "grandfather clause" was to prevent him from ever being on equal par as the poorest of illiterate whites.

This fact had far-reaching ramifications. The intent was to never, ever allow the black man to be politically empowered to abolish slavery in any form or fashion; be it political slavery, economic slavery, or the slavery that comes with being illiterate. The law itself was extremely disheartening to black people.

Not only was this clause designed to imprison black people in a cocoon of ignorance, powerlessness, and self-hatred, but the fomenters orchestrated it so that their children would enter the same prison of darkness and despair upon birth.

The *Concise Columbia Encyclopedia* verifies this by saying that "since African Americans had not yet been enfranchised on [January 1, 1867], the provision effectively barred them from the polls while granting voting rights to poor and illiterate whites." The constitutions of seven Southern states adopted the grandfather clause during the period of 1895 to 1910.

Ku Klux Klan: *a post-Civil War secret society advocating white supremacy; a 20th century secret fraternal group held to confine its membership to American-born white Christians. —Webster's Ninth New Collegiate Dictionary.*

Can you believe this definition? There's nothing about Klansmen being rapists, murderers, and terrorists who hate Jews, certain religious groups and others, but especially blacks! It even gives the impression that the Klan advocated white supremacy only during the "post-Civil War" period!

Encarta (1993), a computerized encyclopedia by Microsoft, is much more honest. It says that the Klan is "a secret terrorist organization that originated in the Southern states during the period of Reconstruction following the American civil war and was reactivated on a wider geographic basis in the 20th century."

The *Oxford English Dictionary* gives some insight as to the background of the Ku Klux Klan by describing the group as follows:

"A widespread secret society, which arose in the Southern States of North America after the civil war of 1861-65, beginning with the effort to overawe the Negro population [and] ... developing a system of political outrage and murder.

"It was revived in 1915 and spread outside the Southern States, terrorizing various ethnic and religious minorities, and acting violent against white Protestants whom they judged to be opposed to their cause.

"Later the society fragmented into several State organizations. The Ku Klux Klan regained strength in the Southern States of the U.S. in the 1950s in opposition to the Civil Rights movement of American Blacks."

"If anyone tries to tell you that blacks shouldn't feel so alone because the Ku Klux Klan dislikes Jews, various other minorities, and even some whites," declares Russell, a black man from South-Central Los Angeles, "don't believe them!"

"The Klan was created by so-called 'Southern gentlemen' who favored the slavery of blacks—not Jews, various other minorities, and especially not whites. They believed so much in the inferiority of African slaves that they were willing to stake their lives on it! And that they did!"

According to Sandra, a black student attending the University of California at Los Angeles, "this insane, diabolical belief " was so ingrained in their psyche that, despite their being on the losing side of the Civil War (and subsequent battles with the U.S. Army), they spread like gangrene beyond the "Southern States" and to this day are bent primarily on the subjugation of the black race.

Martin Luther King Day: *the third Monday in January observed as a legal holiday in some states of the U.S.—Webster's Ninth New Collegiate Dictionary.*

At the time this definition was written "Martin Luther King Day" was celebrated as a legal holiday in the vast majority of states in the U.S.! Yet, the above definition quietly inserts the words, "in some states," as if to diminish its significance.

It seriously downplays this national holiday, and, as if to add insult to injury, the 1994 edition omits the entry altogether.

The *American Heritage Dictionary* treats this holiday more fairly when it says that "Martin Luther King Day" is "the third Monday in January, observed in the United States [not "some states" therein] in commemoration of the birthday of Martin Luther King, Jr."

memsahib: *a white foreign woman of high social status living in India; esp[ecially]: the wife of a British official.—Webster's Ninth New Collegiate Dictionary.*

Why would a word like this be important to the American public? We can only guess. Given the trend of other racist words considered here, it's probably to elevate the white woman (and keep her elevated) no matter where she is in the world.

In fact, the *Oxford English Dictionary* describes a "memsahib" as "a European married lady; also, one who behaves like a European woman."

Make no mistake about it. The white woman from Europe sets the standard for all other women in the world.

By way of contrast, the editors associate black women with the gorilla. (See "gorilla" and "steatopygia" in Chapter III.)

miscegenation: *1864 a mixture of races; esp[ecially]. marriage or cohabitation between a white person and a member of another race.—Webster's Ninth New Collegiate Dictionary.*

This definition isn't entirely honest. What "miscegenation" really means is marriage (or even just sex!) between a white person and a black person. Oh, by the way, "mis-" means "bad," so, "miscegenation" literally means "bad race mixing."

At one time, it was even against the law for a white person to marry a black person. Certain Southern states of the U.S. enacted miscegenation laws that prevented this from happening.

In fact, in 1924, urged on by white supremacists, legislators prohibited whites from marrying anyone with "a single drop of Negro blood," according to the February 13, 1995 issue of *Newsweek*.

And as recently as June 1967, the state of Virginia had a law on its books prohibiting blacks and whites from marrying. And as late as the 1950s the law was used to keep a "salt and pepper" married couple out of the state. Thankfully, the Supreme Court overturned this racist state law.

Instead of giving a full disclosure of these facts, a conspiracy of silence is being perpetrated by a white racist, male-dominated, literary world. The *American Heritage Dictionary* goes along with this charade.

As mentioned earlier, "miscegenation" also means sex between a black person and a white person. Notice what the *Oxford English Dictionary* says under "miscegenation": "Mixture of races; esp[ecially] the sexual union of whites with Negroes." It goes on to mention a book printed in 1864 entitled *Miscegenation: The Theory of the Blending of the Races* which "applied to the American White Man and Negro."

Major dictionaries dance around the real meaning behind "miscegenation." This becomes very obvious when you consider the expression "mixed marriage," which is defined below.

mixed marriage: *(1829) a marriage between persons of different races or religions.—Webster's Ninth New Collegiate Dictionary.*

Lexicographers try to trick us into thinking that "mixed marriage" and "miscegenation" are basically interchangeable terms. Nothing could be farther from the truth. Mixed marriages were okay, AS LONG AS A BLACK MAN WAS NOT MARRYING A WHITE WOMAN!

The expression "mixed marriage" first appeared in print in 1829. It meant marriages primarily between persons of different races, but excluding marriage with a black person. That was taboo. To prevent this from happening, new laws were enacted.

Thirty five years later, in 1864, during the Civil War, miscegenation laws were created and enforced that lasted about 100 years after this *un*Civil War! As stated above, these laws specifically prevented blacks and whites from entering honorable marriage.

It's an exercise in futility when lexicographers grapple to reconcile the contrived differences in definitions between "miscegenation" and "mixed marriage." Though the definition of "mixed marriage" appears innocent, it should clearly state that blacks, for racist reasons, were not lawfully included in such marriages.

neo-Nazi: *a member of a group espousing the programs and policies of Hitler's Nazis.—Webster's Ninth New Collegiate Dictionary.*

Jack Johnson was the first black heavy-weight champ (1908-1915). Any white challenger was called the "Great White Hope." Why? (See "white hope," page 120.)

A member of the Black Panther Party is described as "militant" whereas a Klansman is described as "Christian." (See page 88 under "black panther.")

First of all, "neo" is the Greek word for "new." Once again, the Greeks, perhaps unwittingly this time, have given white racists ammunition against blacks in modern times. (See Chapter III.) But take a close look at the definition and ask yourselves:

Are the "neo-Nazis" depicted as a violent, "militant" group like members of the Black Panther Party are alleged to be? Is it really a "group [just] espousing the pogroms and policies of Hitler's Nazis"?

Well, maybe not saying the truth about the notorious nature of the neo-Nazi party was an oversight on the part of the editors. Let's see what they say about the forerunner of the neo-Nazi party, Hitler's older, original Nazi party. Surely the dictionary will show that the Nazis were vicious and violent.

Webster's Ninth New Collegiate Dictionary and *Webster's Tenth* define the word "Nazi" as "a member of a German fascist party controlling Germany from 1933 to 1945 under Adolf Hitler." What? No indication at all of violence, brutality, intimidation, torture, mutilation, rape, or mass murder?

Try telling that to the families of six million dead Jews, the surviving Jews, Gypsies, homosexuals, Jehovah's Witnesses, and others.

Reportedly, Timothy J. McVeigh, allegedly connected with the April, 1995 bombing of a federal building in Oklahoma City that killed 169 people, is associated with neo-Nazis. In reporting on the claims of an "international conspiracy," the *Los Angeles Times* says "London's Sunday Times reported that the FBI is investigating claims that British and German neo-Nazis helped plan the federal building bombing."

But, according to Webster's, not-so-dangerous neo-Nazis merely confine their activities to rhetoric—or, as the definition indicates: "espousing."

Did you notice, too, that in defining both "neo-Nazi" and "Nazi" the above dictionaries make no mention of antagonist feelings toward "blacks" or "emigrants"? Why, it doesn't even mention that these organizations are white supremacist groups!

reverse discrimination: *(1969) discrimination against whites.—Webster's Ninth New Collegiate Dictionary.*

There's no such thing as "reverse discrimination" against whites. This term is perhaps one of the most notoriously misapplied terms in recent times. To substantiate these bold statements, we'll define "reverse" and "discrimination" in isolation.

"Reverse," in the form of an adjective, means "opposite or contrary to a previous or normal condition." *Webster's Ninth New Collegiate Dictionary* says "discrimination" means "to make a difference in treatment or favor on a basis other than individual merit."

In short, "reverse discrimination" literally means racial discrimination against whites that was previously enforced against blacks.

In the past (as well as in the present), it was normal for whites to be favored for jobs, promotions, and entrance into prestigious schools on the basis of their skin color. Whites were "superior" to blacks who were viewed as being "less than human but more than animal." This was the basis for discriminating against them.

If discrimination is based upon the idea that whites are superior to blacks, then, in order for there to be true "reverse discrimination," the discrimination has to, by definition, be based on the supposition that the black race is superior to the white race. No white institution anywhere, in the history of Europe or America, has ever made this claim!

If blacks are shown preference to whites in the job market, it isn't because of black racial superiority, but, is, in fact, an effort to right the wrongs of the past when whites were shown preference to blacks. (It's a matter of fierce debate as to whether this is the best way to handle past discrimination against blacks, and is beyond the scope of this discussion to make that determination.)

Admittedly, to show a preference based on race, irrespective of the reason, amounts to discrimination. But, the reason, motive, and ability or power to act on that prejudice makes all the difference in the world.

To use a well-known example, suppose a young man shoved a helpless old lady to the ground in the middle of the street. Most people would think this a mean gesture. However, if it were explained that the young man pushed the little old lady out of the way of an oncoming bus that would have surely hit her, then our view of his action immediately changes. Yes, the *reason,* the *motive,* makes all the difference in the world.

Perhaps an even better example is one given by Farai Chideya in her book *Don't Believe The Hype.* She says the following about affirmative action, a subject closely related to "reverse discrimination": "One analogy for the position of whites in affirmative action might be this: Tax time has come, and you mistakenly get an extra fifty dollars in your IRS refund. That same fifty dollars are mistakenly debited from someone else's check. It wasn't your fault the IRS gave you the money.

"Yet even if you didn't realize you'd benefitted from this, the federal government (if vigilant) would still make you give the money back. It's difficult to think about the issue of race in these terms, but in the American job market, being born white is still a clear and unearned advantage. And the value of skin color over a lifetime is far, far more than fifty dollars, as evidenced by the staggering racial homogeneity in the top jobs in American industry."

In conclusion, "reverse discrimination" in the *Oxford English Dictionary* is called, of all things, "positive discrimination." It means "the making of distinctions in favour of groups considered disadvantaged or underprivileged, esp[ecially] in the allocation of resources and opportunities." In other words, it's a "positive" side of "discrimination."

(NOTE: What *Webster's Tenth* Says: It adds the words "as in employment and education.")

tong: *(1883) a secret society or fraternal organization esp[ecially] of Chinese in the U.S. formerly notorious for gang warfare.—Webster's Ninth New Collegiate Dictionary.*

This definition sounds like the one for "Ku Klux Klan" (see above). We note the word "fraternal," just as it appears in that definition. Recall that this word isn't used at all when describing the dictionary entries for "black nationalist" and "Black Panther," as noted above.

Recall, too, that, though the original Black Panther organization is long gone, the Webster's dictionaries don't use the word "formerly" as they do with the above definition of "tong." Besides, the "tong" organization still exists today. (This is a criticism of the above definition, not the tong organization.)

This fact makes it even more nefarious because the editors anxiously state that a specific activity of the "tong" organization, "gang warfare" to be exact, is no longer engaged in. However, the fact that the Black Panther Party was disbanded in 1972 as a "peaceful" fraternal group is lost on the editors.

The Merriam Webster Dictionary (1994), completely eliminates the negative connotation associated with the above word.

It defines "tong" as "a Chinese secret society in the U.S." It doesn't even say they were "formerly notorious for gang warfare."

A familiar question arises: Why doesn't *Webster's Ninth New Collegiate Dictionary* or *Webster's Tenth* mention that the "Ku Klux Klan" is notorious for terrorism and murder? Granted, they say who a "Mohocks" was (a member of white aristocratic gang bangers from 18th century England), but, that was easy. (See "Mohock" in Chapter II.)

The "Mohocks" existed in a different country and century. On the other hand, the editors call "black nationalists," and the now extinct "Black Panthers," "militant" at the drop of a—gun. But they are very reluctant to say anything negative about the "Ku Klux Klan," "skinheads," and "neo-Nazis."

The Webster family of dictionaries seems bent on painting the white man as an angel, while, with the same brush, painting the black race as subhuman "mud people." Yes, they may have looked down on the Chinese and their "tong" organization, but the Chinese are still better than "niggers"!

white man's burden: *the alleged duty of the white peoples to manage the affairs of the less developed nonwhite peoples. —Webster's Ninth New Collegiate Dictionary.*

This is a veiled expression that really says that white people should rule all peoples of the world—but especially black people. Admittedly, the editors give the expression a spin that the originator, Rudyard Kipling, may not have intended.

Kipling, an English novelist, poet, and short-story writer, wrote a poem entitled "The White Man's Burden" in 1899. What he said exactly was: "Take up the White Man's Burden—ye dare not stoop to less." What he meant was that Great Britain should rule the world.

Kipling wrote *The Jungle Book* (1894), *The Second Jungle Book* (1895), *Wee Willie Winkie* (1889), and *Captains Courageous* (1897), all of which were very popular. He was the first writer to receive the Nobel Prize for literature in 1907. Even so, he may well have been an "innocent" racist.

Although Kipling was born in India when it was a British colony, he was all for the colonization of African nations. You'll notice the above definition mentions the supposed duty of white people to help or assist "the less developed nonwhite peoples."

It's more than to help these nonwhite peoples, it's "to govern and impart their culture to nonwhite people," according to the *American Heritage Dictionary*. In other words, whites were to force their culture and impose their will on "the less developed nonwhite peoples."

And how does *Webster's Ninth New Collegiate Dictionary* define the term "non-white"? By way of reminder, it says a nonwhite person is "esp[ecially] one who has African ancestors or the black race." (See "non-white" in Chapter I.)

In reality, when given a full disclosure, the definition of "white man's burden" as interpreted by *Webster's Ninth New Collegiate Dictionary* and the *American Heritage Dictionary* is "the alleged duty of white people to dominate and rob backward, primitive black people of their culture and force the more advanced white culture on them."

In all fairness, though, Kipling himself may have had nobler intentions. He thought the British way was best. Though arrogant, he wanted other peoples around the world to benefit from the best of what the British had to offer.

If you think about the term "white man's burden," Kipling actually felt it was the *unwanted* responsibility of the white man to care for underdeveloped nations of the world, hence the term "burden." Who wants an additional "burden"?

Many, many white people in American and around the world have similar feelings in that they want what's best for everyone, but especially black people who have been victimized by the white powers of the world.

On the other side of the issue, the black man is offended by the execution of Kipling's otherwise noble ideas. He concludes that the white man, among numerous other atrocities, stole the abundant natural resources of the African continent (the richest, most beautiful continent on earth); robbed, enslaved, and "colonized" her children; and then, to add insult to injury, call them the "white man's burden" when they ask back what was illegally stolen from them. This is part of the "black man's burden."

white war: *war without bloodshed; economic warfare. —Oxford English Dictionary*

Well, if you're going to have a "good" war, an "ideal" war, it would of necessity be without bloodshed. It's ideal because no one gets hurt. Here's a good place to stick the word "white." So, now, the best type of war you can possibly have is a "white war." Of course, by implication, the worse kind of war is a "black war."

VI. Racist Religious Words

"The virtuous man hates lying words,
but the wicked man slanders and defames."
—Proverbs 13:5, *The Jerusalem Bible*

✡ ✝

The words in some dictionary definitions are outright lies. These lies, in particular, slander and defame black people. It's especially bad when deceit is carried on in the name of religion. The following few words contain religious overtones that clearly have a racist slant:

assassin: *one of a secret order of Muslims that at the time of the Crusades terrorized Christians and other enemies by secret murder committed under the influence of hashish.—Webster's Ninth New Collegiate Dictionary.*

This word engenders racial and religious prejudice against Arabs and Muslims. In reality, to say that someone was "assassinated" is similar to a buyer saying: "I Jewed him down." "Preplanned murder" and "I bargained" are much more acceptable expressions. Reading this definition could easily cause one to view Muslims suspiciously.

The *American Heritage Dictionary* gives a complete etymology: "At first glance, one would be hard-pressed to find a link between pleasure and the acts of assassins. Such wasn't the case, however, with those who gave us the word assassin.

"They were members of a secret Islamic order originating in the 11th century who believed it was a religious duty to harass and murder their enemies. The most important members of the order were those who actually did the killing.

"Having been promised paradise in return for dying in action, the killers, it is said, were made to yearn for paradise by being given a life of pleasure that included the use of hashish. Hence, the name for the secret order as a whole, hassasin, 'hashish users.' After passing through French or Italian, the word came into English and is recorded in 1603 with reference to the Moslem assassins."

As noted here, the European powers (the French, the Italians, and the English) made it a point to keep the word alive. The *Oxford English Dictionary* agrees by stating that "the [plural] form [was] finally established in the European languages."

European powers readily excuse the terrible crusades where they fought and killed Muslims under the saintly halo of religious piety.

In reality, they fought and killed (or "assassinated") for other than noble reasons, despite the fact that some Arab Muslims were tolerant of Christian practices.

Notice how the *World Book Encyclopedia* explains some of the reasons behind the crusades: "This was a period when Western Europe was expanding its economy and increasing its military forces. The Crusades were a part of a broad Christian expansion movement....Many Crusaders also fought to increase their power, territory, and riches....Most of the new Arab rulers allowed the Christians to visit the shrines....

"Not all the crusaders joined the expeditions for religious reasons. The French knights wanted more land. Italian merchants hoped to expand trade in Middle Eastern ports. Many priests and monks wanted valuable religious relics.

"Large numbers of poor people joined simply to escape the hardships of their normal lives....Some popes used the Crusades for both personal and political gain. However, the Crusades also enriched European life."

Given this information, we can readily understand why the French and Italian "Christians," through their popes, priests, and monks, labeled their Muslims enemies "assassins." They made sure the word would stick.

In actuality, the original Arabic word meant "one who smokes or chews hashish." This didn't suggest at all that all Arabs who smoked or chewed hashish were Moslem fanatics who killed Christians. The so-called Christians, in their medieval Latin, apparently gave the later, more opprobrious, negative connotation to "assassin."

Finally, later in history, the "Christian" Europeans did something worse than what the Moslem "assassins" did, but the Europeans innocuously called themselves, not "assassins," but "Crusaders" (from *crux* or *cross*) and/or "colonists."

caste: *one of the hereditary social classes in Hinduism that restrict the occupation of their members and their association with the members of other castes ... a system of rigid social stratification characterized by hereditary status, endogamy, and social barriers sanctioned by custom, law, or religion.—Webster's Ninth New Collegiate Dictionary.*

"Caste" qualifies as a racist word for a couple of reasons: (1) It's of Greek origin. As has been shown above, the Greeks had mixed feelings, more on the negative side, toward Africans. These feelings were expressed, not only in Greek words, but also in Greek legends. (See Chapter III.) (2) The Portuguese adopted and passed on the word. Not only did the Portuguese initiate the slave trade, their word "casta" means "race, lineage, ... pure, chaste." In other words, a pure, chaste white race. (Incidentally, "chaste" is "caste" with an "h" after the "c.")

When you hear the word "caste" you think immediately of India and her Hindu religion. Even though the caste system is officially outlawed, it's as alive and well as is officially outlawed racial discrimination is in the United States.

Some believe that it's no coincidence that dark-skinned people are invariably in the lower castes in both American and Indian societies.

In further proof that the United States has its own form of a caste system, the above definition says that this caste system is "a system of rigid social stratification [strictly defined race categories with the white race at the top] characterized by hereditary status [if you're of Negro or African ancestry you're at the bottom], endogamy ["marriage in a specific group as required by custom or law," (Webster's)], and social barriers [like glass ceilings, job and housing discrimination] sanctioned by custom, law, or religion."

Racial discrimination is now, and has been, customary in the United States; is now, and has been, lawful in the United States; is now, and has been, part of the so-called "Christian" religion in this land which alleges to have based its very constitution upon the Judeo-Christian ethic. (Incidentally, the Ku Klux Klan call themselves "Christians.")

The *Oxford English Dictionary* tells us that "caste" is of Spanish and Portuguese origin and basically means "race, lineage, breed." It quotes one lexicographer (Diez) as saying it means "pure or unmixed (stock or breed)....For Spanish caste, applied in South America, to the several mixed breeds between Europeans, Indians, and Negroes." ("Pariah": "untouchable" black low caste member.)

Ku Klux Klan: *a post-Civil War secret society advocating white supremacy; a 20th century secret fraternal group held to confine its membership to American-born white Christians. —Webster's Ninth New Collegiate Dictionary.*

A Christian is a follower of Jesus Christ. Can you imagine Jesus raping, torturing, lynching, mutilating, or murdering blacks and others?

The original Klan was organized in Pulaski, Tennessee, on December 24, 1865, by six former Confederate army officers who gave their society a name adapted from the Greek word *kuklos* ("circle").

Apparently these "former Confederate army officers" knew that the ancient Greeks looked down on the more technologically advanced Africans and chose a word meaning "circle" in the Greek "New Testament" as a basis for the name of their illicit, "Christian," organization.

Webster's Ninth New Collegiate Dictionary assures us that it's a fraternal group of American-born white followers of the Lord Jesus Christ himself.

WASP or Wasp: *[white Anglo-Saxon Protestant] (1960): an American of Northern European and esp[ecially] British stock and of Protestant background...a member of the dominant and the most privileged class of people in the U.S.—sometimes used disparagingly.—Webster's Ninth New Collegiate Dictionary.*

The editors tell us that a WASP is "a member of a dominant ... class of people in the U.S.," but they fail to mention just who is dominated over. American history tells us that whites dominated and enslaved blacks.

The things so-called Christians did in the name of God and the Bible were unimaginable. And, yet, these Protestants (and Catholics!) perpetrated frauds with respect to slavery and then tried to hide behind the Bible to justify their heartless actions.

These facts are curiously absent from Webster's definition of WASP. Even so, the black man (and innocent whites!) has grown tired of being stung by this kind of "WASP."

white father: *a white man regarded as protecting or controlling people of another race; a member of the society of Missionaries of Africa, a Roman Catholic order founded in Algiers in 1868.—The Oxford English Dictionary.*

The idea of one race "controlling people of another race" appeals to the white racist. Most people aren't aware that such a term as "white father" even exists. It does. And it's complete with an ugly definition.

By the above definition, the founding fathers of the United States of America were all, not only white, but 'white fathers.' These whites of European ancestry are also the architects of the Constitution, the oldest legal document of its kind in the world.

All that is just fine, except that America has been anything but fatherly to minorities—especially to blacks, the largest minority group in the country. The white fathers have consistently controlled blacks; some of them even owning black slaves.

Religion's role hasn't been a pretty one when it comes to black slavery. While Catholic priests are called "father," some of those living in the days of the slave trade could more appropriately be called 'white fathers.'

No wonder the Pope (a form of "Papa" or "Father") recently apologized for the Church's role in the African slave trade.

VII. Racist Words—A General Listing

" Untruth and the lying word
put far away from me."
—Proverbs 30:8, *New World Translation*

☹

No one wants to be lied to. Who wants "untruths" told about him? Imagine if everyone lied, all the time, to everyone else. The world would be a mess. Actually, the world is a mess, and one of the things that contributes to this messed up world is the "lying word" we find in the dictionary. Just look at these lies, half-truths, and omissions:

aboriginal: *(1667) being the first of its kind present in a region and often primitive in comparison with more advanced types.—Webster's Ninth New Collegiate Dictionary.*

"[M]ore advanced types"? What could this possibly mean? Well, let's discuss the word's origin first. If you're like most people, you're probably thinking about the Australian Aborigines. Actually, the word is derived from a Latin noun that literally means "from the beginning." In other words, it means people who were in a land, country or region, "from the beginning."

The first part of the above definition is completely acceptable for it's devoid of any racist overtones. It simply states: "being the first of its kind present in a region." It's the part after that that's disturbing.

We encounter the problem with the next clause, "and often primitive in comparison with more advanced types."

Regrettably, the offensive latter part of the definition swings the door open for the "more advanced types" (a subtle reference to European colonists) to come in and conquer, rape, decimate and pillage the indigenous people and their land.

The *Oxford English Dictionary* is more pointed when it defines "aboriginal" as "[d]welling in a country before the arrival of later (European) colonists."

Even *Webster's Ninth New Collegiate Dictionary* admits the following under the word aborigine: "An aboriginal inhabitant esp[ecially] as contrasted with an invading or colonizing people."

They cleverly left out the word "European" in this definition. But, the *Oxford English Dictionary* honestly inserts it. Yes, the offending "invading or colonizing people" were from Europe.

(NOTE: What *Webster's Tenth* Says: It removes the offending words "and often primitive in comparison with more advanced types.")

argot: (1860): *an often more or less secret vocabulary and idiom peculiar to a particular group <the American Negro has ... developed his own argot, partly to put the white man off, partly to put him down—Daniel Stern>—Webster's Ninth New Collegiate Dictionary*.

Note the negative, divisive, inflammatory example used by the editors. While North American blacks have long had their "jive" talk or "black English" (discussed in Chapter II), other races and cultures in America have had a language peculiarly their own.

Unfortunately, "the American Negro" is suspiciously singled out in the above example complete with its racist overtones. That the word "argot" carries with it a negative connotation is born out by the *Oxford English Dictionary*: "The jargon, slang, or peculiar phraseology of a class, orig[inally] that of thieves and rogues."

In other words, it isn't at all difficult to conceive that "the American Negro" generally fits into the same category as do "thieves and rogues," according to *Webster's Ninth New Collegiate Dictionary*.

(NOTE: What *Webster's Tenth* Says: It changes the above example to the following: "[S]hoved into a taxi by a porter whose argot I couldn't understand—Allen Tate." Unfortunately, it may still be a slight to the black man, who, at that time, made up most of porterdom.)

boy: *a male servant—sometimes taken offensively.—Webster's Ninth New Collegiate Dictionary.*

For a black man, this word is not just "sometimes taken offensively," it's probably offensive most, if not all the time, if a white person says it.

The *Oxford English Dictionary* defines "boy" as "a servant, slave." In South Africa, when apartheid was in effect, a boy was "a Coloured or Native labourer or servant of any age...a Cape Coloured man or boy." Yes, "boy" meant subservient black man.

American history tells us that the "Negro" slave was called "boy." It was meant to be humiliating, or, at the very least, a reminder that he was a dependant in a one-sided patristic relationship with the white man. *Webster's Ninth New Collegiate Dictionary* conveniently leaves this tidbit out.

Not surprisingly, European powers are responsible for this racist word. The *American Heritage Dictionary* gives this revealing origin of the word "boy": "Middle English *boi,* possibly from Old French *embuie,* servant, past participle of *embuier,* to fetter." This is consistent since, as we all know, slaves were fettered.

The dictionary compares this monkey to the black man. Never is any white man likened to an animal in a derogatory sense. (See "sambo" on page 50.)

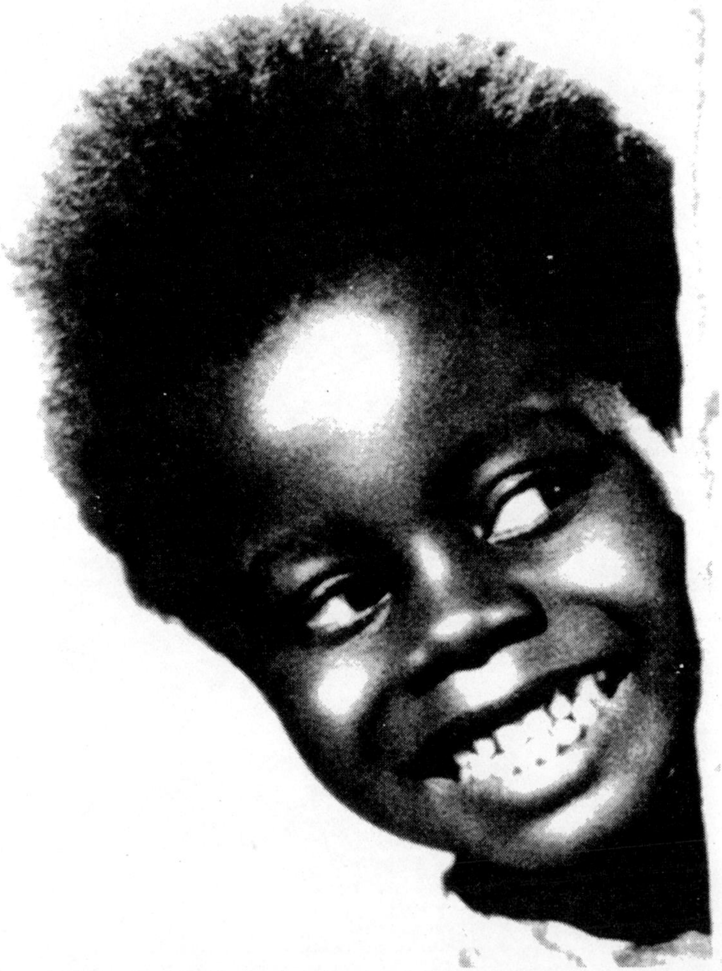

Buckwheat was the classic example of what the dictionary disparagingly calls black men. (See "wooly-headed" on page 64.)

No matter how old a male slave was, he was still a "boy" to his masters. Men of color today will readily tell you that they are still shackled or fettered, regardless of age, by the mores of white society.

Esperanto: *based upon "the chief European languages." —Webster's Ninth New Collegiate Dictionary.*

"Why does it have to be the 'chief European languages'? What makes these so superior?" asked Charlene, a black high school English teacher. "Based upon the racist elements in these languages, Esperanto is bound to be the culmination of the worst of these languages," she mused.

Charlene's concern is that, since, for the most part, European languages denigrate the black man, why would Esperanto be any different? The last thing the black man wants to see is anything "based upon the chief European languages."

holler: (1825) *a freely improvised American Negro work song.—Webster's Ninth New Collegiate Dictionary.*

Did you notice? "[H]oller" is an "American Negro work song." Frankly, this is a word born out of slavery. "Yes, black folks are happiest when they are working and singing. That's why they do it so well." This was the observation of Jim, an otherwise well adjusted white man. A disturbing stereotype, indeed.

Upon closer examination you'll find that the slaves were doing much more than singing when they worked. *The World Book Encyclopedia* gives us a brief history of "calypso," a type of singing and/or music:

"Calypso originated in the songs of African slaves who worked in the plantation fields of Trinidad. They were forbidden to talk to each other, and used calypso to communicate feelings and information. To fool their masters, they sang in a French-Creole dialect called patois."

The slave masters feared that if their slaves spoke at length with each other they would plan either a rebellion or an escape. They weren't singing because they were happy to be working on a plantation. They were communicating, either with God or with each other.

The inhumanities carried out in the name of the Black African slave trade would have made anyone want to holler! That is to say, "scream" or "shout" in disgust.

juba: *[origin unknown] (1834): a dance of Southern plantation Negroes accompanied by complexly rhythmic hand clapping and slapping of the knees and thighs.—Webster's Ninth New Collegiate Dictionary.*

This definition appears inoffensive at first glance. In fact, it seems complimentary. But it carries with it subtle stereotypes. It fosters the idea that dancing is what black people are really good at.

Additionally, it suggests that "Southern plantation Negroes" were tickled pink to be slaves. They were so delighted with their plight that you could hardly restrain them from dancing about in a 'complex rhythmic' way.

"Now, it could be that certain whites are jealous of the soulful moves blacks have been blessed with," says Tony, a black music instructor. The inability of most white people to dance as rhythmatically complex as blacks is called, by the *Oxford English Dictionary*, a "white joke." It officially defines it as the "name of some dance."

Despite the dancing ability of blacks, they haven't been able to dance their way out from under the burden of racism. In all fairness, though, a few of the best tap dancers in the history of tap dancing were white.

maroon: *a fugitive Negro slave of the West Indies and Guiana in the 17th and 18th centuries; also; a descendant of such a slave.—Webster's Ninth New Collegiate Dictionary.*

Does the world look on maroons (descendants of slaves) as people having to pay a debt to society? Why is the distinction made between a descendant of a slave and a descendant of a runaway slave? The *Concise Columbia Encyclopedia* offers us an interesting word history:

"The history of the word maroon, which we associate with desert islands, takes us back to the days of slavery, when the noun maroon was a term in English for a Black person who lived in the mountains and forests of Dutch Guiana (Suriname) and the West Indies, a term that is still used in parts of the Caribbean.

"These were plantation slaves who had run away to live free in uncultivated parts. The English word is taken from the French word maroon, 'runaway Black slave,' which in turn was an alteration of American Spanish cimarrón, meaning 'runaway slave.'

"Cimarrón is perhaps from cima, 'summit.' Having come into English (first recorded in 1666), maroon took on a life of its own and came to be used as a verb meaning 'to be lost in the wilds,' from which our sense 'to put ashore on a deserted island or coast' evolved."

What the racist white man is saying to the black man by way of the above definition is: "Remember where you're from, nigger!" The point being made here is this: "You're black already, but, aside from that, you are the descendant of a law-breaking, ungrateful runaway slave."

As if being black isn't bad enough in a world where the only superpower (whose policies influence how other nations view black people) has a tragic history with respect to the slave trade, an additional onus is put on the backs of blacks in the Americas whose forefathers were "maroons." (See also "contraband" in Chapter II.)

niggard: *a meanly covetous and stingy person.—Webster's Ninth New Collegiate Dictionary.*

Believe it or not, this word is still completely acceptable in the English language, irrespective of its kinship (or at least disturbingly comparable vocalization) to the "N" word.

In fact, there's more to it besides the hauntingly similar vocalization. The *Oxford English Dictionary* says that "Nigger" is a "dial[lectical] variant of NIGGARD." In other words, "niggard" and "nigger" are definitely related, although most dictionaries won't acknowledge this fact.

If you feel that a big issue is being made over nothing, consider these two questions: Although the word 'niggard' means "stingy person," doesn't it sound like "nigger"? If you disagree with this, would you be willing to call a stingy stranger, who happens to be black, a "niggard"?

There are plenty of other English words that do the job: "penury," "parsimony," and "stingy" to name a few. So, it's too bad that the editors weren't "niggardly" in their use of this word. It would have been far better if they "stingily" kept the word "niggard" out of the dictionary.

white hope: *a white contender for a boxing championship held by a black; also, one who is felt to represent whites; one from whom much is expected; esp[ecially] a person undertaking a difficult task.—Webster's Ninth New Collegiate Dictionary.*

Is there a dictionary entry for "black hope"? And, if so, would it be defined as "one from whom little is expected?" or, "a person undertaking an easy task?"

The *Oxford English Dictionary* gives us a little more background by defining "white hope" as follows: "A white boxer who might beat Jack Johnson, the first Black to be world heavyweight champion (1908-15); hence, a person who, or a thing which, it is hoped will achieve much or on whom or which hopes are centered."

So, anything good, any remedy, any solution, is to be associated with the white man beating up on the bad, problematic black man? Perhaps to white racists, but, thankfully, not most white people.

white knight: *one that comes to the rescue; esp[ecially] a corporation invited to buy out a second corporation in order to prevent an undesired takeover by a third; one that champions a cause.—Webster's Ninth New Collegiate Dictionary.*

Though this gets tiresome, again, our hero, our knight in shining armor, is white. We are encouraged to look to the white man as our hero—our savior. And, yes, corporate America is dominated by male whites. They are disproportionately represented when compared to the rank and file. White men make up 95 percent of America's top executives while they make up 43 percent of the work force.

white slave: *(1857) a woman or girl held unwillingly for purposes of commercial prostitution.—Webster's Ninth New Collegiate Dictionary.*

Since black female slaves were regularly raped by white male plantation slave owners, white women who are forced into prostitution are compared to black female slaves of America's early years. You'll notice this term appeared in print a few years before the Civil War (1857).

The *Oxford English Dictionary* defines "white slave" as "a white person...who is, or is treated like, a slave." To distinguish white women from the black women, someone came up with the term "white slave" which is both racist and sexist.

Although this term showed up in print in the late 19th century, there's reason to believe that it showed up with reference to Africans in the early 16th century. Not surprisingly, the Portuguese, pioneers of the slave trade, were behind white slavery, which at that time included men.

According to *The People's Chronology* (1992), "the Portuguese [captured] Zafi in Morocco and [began] commerce in captive Moors, Berbers, and Jews. Many [were] women, all [were] called white slaves."

There's an ironic twist to the usage of the term "white slave," or a derivative thereof. When the heavyweight champion of the world, Jack Johnson (see "white hope" above) dated a white woman and had his way with her, he was accused of being a pimp. This so enraged white America that Congress, on June 25, 1910, conjured up a law against what Johnson was perceived to have done.

According to *The People's Chronology*, "the Mann White Slave Traffic Act passed by Congress ... discourages interstate transportation of women for immoral purposes. Newspaper stories about prizefighter Jack Johnson have inspired passage of the law."

You wonder why there wasn't a law against raping black women, especially by white men, enacted by congress during this very same time period.

white son: *a beloved or favourite son; a boy or man who is especially favoured or petted.*—The *Oxford English Dictionary*

They've given the term "favorite son" another name. They've maneuvered "white" into it. So, in the Biblical account of Jacob ("Israel") and his twelve sons, Joseph could rightly, according to the above definition, be called the "white son." The remaining eleven sons, let the racists tell it, could rightly be called "black sheep" of the family.

The Antidote

At the beginning of Chapter One, "Racism and Black Essence," a question from thousands of years ago was asked: "Does not the ear test words and the mouth taste its food?" These words are recorded in the Bible book of Job. We were encouraged to "taste" dictionary words before we consume them. If we've partaken of the poison already, fast action is required. We can combat the toxicity already in our intellectual system by drinking the antidote of "education." In so doing, we will be well on our way to recovery.

Chapter Two, "Every Day Racist Slurs," started out with an age-old question from the same book of Job. "How long will you exhaust me and pulverize me with words?" As was noted at the beginning of this chapter, words can hurt, bruise, and scar. We've all experienced, at one time or another, the cutting effect of words. They were thrown our way with such force and velocity that they crushed our "emotional" bones. We can take heart though. The soothing balm of truth cannot only relieve the pain caused by dictionary words, but can mend badly broken "emotional" bones.

Chapter Three, "The Greek Origin of Racist Words," started out with some solid, practical advice. "Do not give your heart to all the words that people may speak," the wise man Solomon tells us. This admonition is as sound today as it was in ancient times. As discussed in Chapter Three, the usage of racially biased words reaches as far back as the ancient Greeks. So, the exercise of offensive, derogatory words is not new. Surely we have all been victimized by cruel, bad, untrue sayings, regardless of whether the person saying these things meant to do us harm. And even if they do mean them, wisdom dictates that we should not 'give our heart to' (or believe in) the harsh words spoken. While we cannot control the person leveling the offensive words against us, hopefully we can control our reaction.

In Chapter Four, "Racist Words: Science and Medicine," an ancient voice told us that "[T]he simple man believes every word he hears [while] a clever man understands the need for proof." Man has yet to find a cure for the real disease behind all of the rhetoric that exists in some dictionary definitions. With a sinister posture, the diseased mind of the white racist lurks below the surface of dictionary definitions. Ironically, in other cases, it's a mixture of innocence and ignorance beneath the definition.

The white racist is especially dangerous when he has the power of the pen; the power to influence (maybe "infect" is the better word) the thinking of others. Surely, the "vaccine" of accurate knowledge is the first step in remedying such a perplexing problem.

In Chapter Five, "Politics, The Law, and Racism," the Wisdom Of The Ages continues by saying: "A soft answer turns away wrath, but harsh words cause quarrels." More recently, the late Dr. Martin Luther King, Jr. said "you can't legislate what's in a man's heart." Unfortunately, though, a racist can legislate what is in his heart and even incorporate it in the dictionary.

Complex social issues involving race relations in the U.S. confound the best political minds modern-day society has to offer. The quarreling and quandaries continue. In democratic societies, voting is often a choice between the lesser of two evils. Justice and fairness are distressingly infrequent. Even the best political systems are flawed.

Despite these realities, we can enjoy a measure of happiness, even under these circumstances. Have we ***ever*** been happy in our lives? If ***any*** of us have, this proves that a measure of happiness is possible, irrespective of the inequities of an imperfect society.

It behooves us to work within the bounds of the inescapable imperfections of the system. Make hope real. Relief is bound to come. We shouldn't take ourselves too seriously, and we should simply love our fellow man—regardless of his color.

In Chapter Six, "Racist Religious Words," we heard a voice echoing down through the corridors of time, saying: "The virtuous man hates lying words, but the wicked man slanders and defames."

As noted in this chapter, no one wants to be lied to or defamed. It's morally wrong. For this reason and others, victims of lies and defamation have a recourse. People are sued regularly for slander, defamation of character, infliction of emotional harm, and intentional infliction of emotional harm.

In theory, our constitutional laws—based on the Judeo-Christian ethic—protect and aid the downtrodden, the disadvantaged, the weak. Shouldn't the beliefs and actions of Jews and Christians be consistent with these laws?

If you're Jewish, the Hebrew Bible tells you that God is on the side of the fatherless boy, the widow, the poor, and the afflicted. He demanded no less from the Israelites. They were to aid, whenever possible, the less fortunate. In American society African Americans are the less fortunate ones. Even the dictionary singles them out for unwarranted criticism.

If you're a Christian, you have preserved for you a record of what Jesus, your Master, did when he walked the earth. How did he feel about the lowly ones? It's hard to imagine Jesus hating people solely on the basis of their dark skin; especially since his skin was no doubt brownish in color. Instead, according to the Gospels, he died for everyone.

If you have any belief in some benevolent Supreme Being, you must know that he will rectify matters in his own good time.

But, whether you're religiously inclined or not, a sense of fairness and justice are inherent in human nature. Being aware that mainly blacks have been the brunt of racially biased statements in the dictionary, and that we all have been duped by these statements, should make us more sensitive to each others feelings. This, to be sure, is a start in the right direction.

One well-known poet from yesteryear made this request of God: "Untruth and the lying word put far away from me." At the start of Chapter Seven, "Racist Words—A General Listing," we talked about lies. These can rip to pieces the fabric of any society, no matter how advanced, and can eat away at the very infrastructure of civilization. When the entire world has been lied to about a certain group of people (blacks), and the lies have been believed and acted upon, it makes for, at the very least, a bewildering situation.

But, there's reason for optimism. Once we are cognizant of the actual existence of half-truths and prevarication in what is the second most fundamental book in our society, the dictionary, (the Bible is first) we can address the distortions. The present work has attempted to identify and zero in on these terms.

Not only is it my intention to "search and destroy" the racist thoughts behind these words, I hope to destroy the misimpressions and erroneous ideas of blacks that these words have either created, or supported in the minds of innocent blacks, whites, and others.

It is not the intent of this book to start a war of words. Wars, fights, mutual animosities, and the like are things we can certainly do without. Instead of engaging in such, we can all do our part in coming to a better understanding of each other's race, no matter what that race may be. Finally, here's something you can do personally: tell dictionary editors to stop using wicked words as weapons, and, for a change, promote peace through truth and honesty.

" Remind them of these facts and charge them in the presence of God to indulge in no wars of words; it helps no one and it completely upsets the listeners."

—2 Timothy 2:14, *The Modern Language Bible*

SUBJECT INDEX

Galeano, Eduardo p. 8

blessed